CHINNERY
The man and the legend

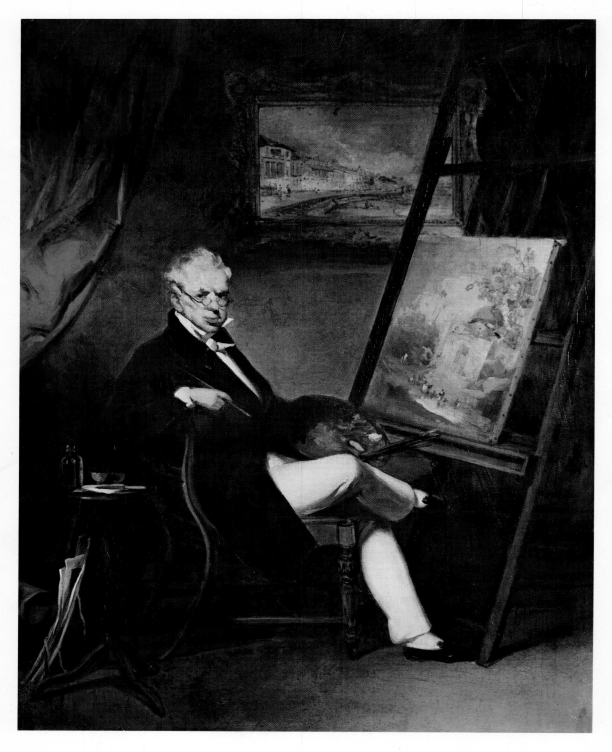

George Chinnery, self-portrait

II

CHINNERY
The man and the legend

by

Robin Hutcheon

with a chapter on Chinnery's shorthand
by
Geoffrey W. Bonsall

South China Morning Post, Limited.
1975

Published and Printed *by* South China Morning Post, Limited.

Hongkong

Foreword

NINETEEN seventy four marked the 200th anniversary of the birth of George Chinnery and in Hongkong and Macau the bicentenary kindled new interest in the works and life of this expatriate British artist.

Chinnery is as much appreciated by experts in India, Hongkong, the United States and Ireland, as he is in his own native Britain. He left England in 1802 at the age of 28 never to return, but he studied under such masters as Sir Joshua Reynolds and must be classified with British portrait and landscape painters of that era. Although he regarded himself as one of the great artists of the time he is now considered by most critics to be a respected minor master with a number of outstanding portraits, landscapes and water colours to his credit.

Chinnery deserves a good biography. Many have said this. However a good deal of research into his life and work is still going on. More needs to be done to fill in the large gaps at various periods of his life. His correspondence, the subject of a recent study by Mr Richard Ormond, Assistant Keeper of the National Portrait Gallery in London, has thrown more light on his methods and techniques in oil and water-colour painting as well as landscapes and miniatures. It has also proved to be a revealing source of information on his talent for teaching and indeed Chinnery began, with the help of one of his pupils in Calcutta, making notes for what was apparently intended to be a treatise on painting.

An even more exacting study is being made of Chinnery's shorthand by Mr Geoffrey W. Bonsall, Director of the Hongkong University Press, who is trying to reconstruct some of Chinnery's life from the thousands of drawings he left, most of which were meticulously dated and in many cases carried additions of shorthand notes. Curiously very little interest was shown in Chinnery's shorthand until recent times and there was at least one collector who thought that it might have been Tamil script instead of Gurney shorthand.

It does seem desirable, however, that following the 200th anniversary of his birth, an attempt should be made to bring together what others have discovered in the course of patient study and research over the last 50 years and to try and set the record straight on the known episodes of his life.

If he was not considered one of the great masters of the last century his reputation has been steadily improving with the years. At least that judgment holds good for his best portraits and some of his miniatures. He did better as a painter of water-colours and sketched prolifically in pencil and ink; his draughtsmanship is particularly appreciated by experts. It is true to say, however, that his sketches until recent years have been ignored except by private collectors who could not afford an oil. These possess simplicity, charm and freshness and vividly portray the places and people of Chinnery's time. They also reveal his methods and how he prepared studies for his pictures.

Living in an age before the advent of photography, Chinnery left us intimate glimpses of life as it was in India, Macau, Canton and Hongkong in the assortment of paintings, drawings, sketches, letters, notes and anecdotes which survive. For this reason he holds a valued, indeed unique place in the history of British contacts with Asia in the last century.

However, he is a man about whom legend has spun a web of fantasy, and this has in turn been embellished by novelists, journalists and historians, creating a travesty of the real Chinnery. He has been credited – or rather miscredited – with the works of at least a dozen inferior artists who have been placed together as members of a supposed "Chinnery school" as if his copiers or rivals were his equals. This has greatly retarded and misdirected a true assessment of his artistry.

He has been hailed as the innovator of the western school of painting in China and although his influence was important during the 27 years he lived in Macau, and continued to be after his death, he was in fact only one of many British or European artists who visited the Far East in the century prior to his death.

He has been described by the authors of one book as "the artist of the China coast"[1] when in fact there is no evidence that he travelled further afield than Macau, the Pearl River delta, Canton and Hongkong – to the latter only briefly, incidentally – a small triangle 70 miles on each leg and 40 miles at the base. It is time therefore to look at Chinnery's life and artistic achievements in some detail to see what was his greatest contribution to his profession and to the history of his time.

He was the most prominent and best known illustrator and painter in the western style in Asia and the Far East in the early to middle part of the 19th century. He had an eye for detail and colour and an ability to portray scenes far more ably and realistically than any of his local contemporaries, whether in Macau, Canton or India. He more than filled in for the modern photographers who have now made Hongkong, for instance, one of the most over-photographed places in the world. Had he been born a generation or so later he might have made his mark as a cartoonist because of his facility for depicting scenes and people with a few quick deft strokes.

Thanks to Chinnery, we know what Macau, parts of Canton and Hongkong looked like in the first half of the 19th century. We have some superb paintings of the environs of Macau and life on the busy Pearl River which links Canton with the sea. All these have given us a much more vivid impression of the people of that time and their way of life. Chinnery, however, saw life from the outside. At no time could he be said to have "lived native." He remained very much the 19th century Englishman abroad, though because the Chinese in Macau and Canton lived their lives so very much in the open and because Chinnery was such an assiduous and talented artist he gave us an extraordinarily diverse record of life.[2]

Where Chinnery's record ends it has been continued, partly by the photographer and in more recent years by professional painters and film-makers – though whether Chinnery's drawings have ever been excelled is doubtful.

He was far from being the first western painter to come to the Orient. About a century earlier Brother Guiseppe Castiglione had lived and worked in China and earned the admiration of the great Ching emperor, Chien Lung, for his paintings in the Chinese style.

There was another Jesuit painter named Sichelbarth and together with a lay brother named Denis Attiret they enjoyed imperial favour in Peking. These men have left us equally remarkable impressions of their life in China though their paintings and style made little impression on artists, except in the capital, and even this was transitory.

Chinnery and his contemporaries did make a definite impression on Chinese artists and while it can be argued that when he arrived in 1825 the Chinese at various levels were already familiar with the western style and more receptive to western influence – if only for commercial reasons – Chinnery succeeded in setting a standard that has not been equalled in portraits and sketches to this day.

There are many artists in Hongkong who paint the same scenes that first charmed Chinnery – junks, fishing boats, the wrinkled faces of old men, gamblers, ironmongers, street barbers, women carrying babies on their backs, sampan girls, village scenes and farm animals, though none with such vitality, accuracy or quality, and we can only regret that someone of like talent is not able to represent the current scene with his mastery of draughtsmanship.

But no less important than his influence and style of painting and sketching, were the historical subjects he painted – people like Howqua, the well-known Hong merchant, Chinese and Indian dignitaries, western merchants and officials.

A subject of endless fascination to Chinnery was himself and one of his masterpieces is his self-portrait which is in London's National Portrait Gallery in Trafalgar Square; he painted many other self-portraits at various times in his life, and a separate chapter has been devoted to these.

From his pictures we can glean a little of Chinnery's own life and habits in Macau and Canton. Certainly although he enjoyed the patronage of wealthy and influential men, his Macau period was less rewarding financially than his India days, and he must have endured a far more modest and lonely existence, particularly in his later years.

The market was far narrower than in Calcutta and Dacca and he was perpetually dependent on the goodwill of the small foreign community and the officers of naval and merchant ships which visited the area. He painted many of them in his 27 years in Macau as well as some of the more notable visitors who passed through Canton and Macau.

His pictures varied between outstanding in the case of those who interested him, to indifferent in the case of those who failed to make an impression on him, although his admirers would dispute this statement by questioning whether those of a lower standard were in fact his work. Human nature being what it is, however, it would have been difficult for such a prolific painter as Chinnery to have maintained a uniformly high standard of excellence. Several writers, moreover, report that he would sometimes leave work "unfinished" and in Calcutta after his departure for Macau in 1825 as many as 50 incomplete canvases were found in his studio.[3] Once again present-day students of his work consider that the attribution of unfinished pictures to Chinnery has been done by "dealers who have neither technical nor historical knowledge."[4]

In Macau and Canton he found himself being undercut in price particularly in his later years by a stylish Chinese painter named Lamqua who, in addition to his own very attractive pictures, turned out others on an assembly line basis in a workshop in Canton.

Chinnery, however, was much more than a popular painter. His personal charm was legendary and as a garrulous eccentric he was a well-known figure in the social life of the foreign community and in consequence was rarely short of an invitation to breakfast or dinner.

He came to China not to paint new scenes but to escape a staggering burden of debts in India and a marital breakdown, aggravated as it was by the death of his son. His output during the Macau period, both in oils and sketches, was prodigious though increasingly

Chinnery's pencil and ink drawings became the dominant element in his work and it is these that today command increasing attention and interest.

This book is based on a series of ten articles the author wrote at the beginning of 1974 for the Sunday Post-Herald in Hongkong and which in turn were based on extensive interviews and correspondence with Chinnery scholars such as Dr J. R. Jones, the former legal adviser to the Hongkong and Shanghai Banking Corporation and the person largely responsible for encouraging the Bank to assemble its post-war collection of Chinnery paintings and sketches, Mr Geoffrey W. Bonsall, Director of the Hongkong University Press, who has made a long and detailed study of Chinnery's works and particularly his shorthand, Mr Richard Ormond of London, Father Manuel Teixeira, the Macau historian, and others who have helped to shake the Chinnery sieve to separate the mass of myth and legend from the nuggets of accepted facts.

I am particularly indebted to Mr Bonsall, Dr Jones, Mr Ormond and Mr Francis B. Lothrop, Trustee of the Peabody Museum in Salem, Massachusetts, for reading the text of my articles and for making many criticisms and suggestions.

For presentation in book form the articles have been completely revised and expanded with additional material, and again read by both Mr Bonsall and Mr Lothrop whose suggestions and criticisms have proved most helpful.

The Hongkong and Shanghai Banking Corporation and the Hongkong City Museum and Art Gallery have kindly given me access to their collections and allowed me to take photographs. Galleries and museums overseas have provided other photographs of Chinnery paintings and sketches.

The co-operation, advice and encouragement I have received from many people is deeply appreciated. Without it this book could not have been written.

This is incidentally one of at least three new publications dealing with various aspects of Chinnery's work and together with the important research now being undertaken by scholars they demonstrate a welcome interest by this generation in his achievements.

On May 30, 1974, Macau commemorated Chinnery's bicentenary. The ceremony consisted of a short ecumenical service at the Chapel in the Old Protestant Cemetery where Chinnery is buried, the mounting and unveiling of a plaque on Chinnery's monument by the Governor of Macau, General Nobre de Carvalho, the opening of an exhibition of Chinnery's works at the Museum Luis de Camoens, with a catalogue in Portuguese and Chinese prepared by Mr Luis Gonzaga Gomes, and the renaming of a street after the artist. Later in the year the Macau Government issued a single stamp commemorating the bicentenary, featuring Chinnery's 1840 self-portrait.

The wording of the plaque for Chinnery's grave was prepared by Sir Lindsay Ride, former Vice-Chancellor of the University of Hongkong, who has laboured for years to restore the headstones in the cemetery and has undertaken extensive research on those buried there.

The citation to Chinnery at this ceremony was read by the author and translated into Portuguese by Fr. Teixeira.

— R. H.

This oil painting of Mrs Eustace, the grandmother of the artist's wife, was painted in Dublin during Chinnery's residence there between 1796 and 1802.

The Earl of Minto, Governor-General of India from 1807-1813; this painting, attributed to George Chinnery, was presented by the Fourth Earl to Hawick Town Council in 1893.

Index

Colour plates

1

A mark of genius

I F George Chinnery was not born with a silver spoon in his mouth, it could be said that he had a paintbrush or pencil in his hand from an early age.

His father, William, was a talented amateur painter who had exhibited two pictures at the Free Society of Artists in 1764 and 1766. His grandfather was a shorthand expert and writing master who distinguished himself by publishing in 1750 a book entitled "Writing and Drawing made Easy, Amusing and Instructive."[1] Grandfather William's expertise at shorthand – the Gurney system – is noteworthy because a distinctive feature of George Chinnery's sketches and illustrations is his frequent use of shorthand to make notes on colours and particular features of his drawings, or refer to background details.

Whether George studied shorthand under his grandfather or picked it up by himself is not known. Nor is much known of his early education though his family background is clearly middle class, for his father has been described as an East India merchant with an interest in a factory in Cuddalore in the Madras Presidency. It would appear therefore that the Chinnerys enjoyed a fairly comfortable existence.

Legends grew up with Chinnery, even about the day he was born. Careless research by earlier critics and writers suggested he was a native of Dublin and his birthdate was confused with that of his father in such a way that the Macau legend that he was 100 years old at the time of his death was given some support.[2] So let us begin by putting the record straight.

George Chinnery was born in London on January 5, 1774, and he was the sixth child and fifth son.[3] His mother was Elizabeth Bassett and her surname was passed to George's eldest surviving brother, William Bassett Chinnery.

The family residence was at 4 Gough Square, Fleet Street, better known as one of the haunts of the Scottish diarist, James Boswell, and also the home of Dr Johnson. The square survives today midway between Chancery Lane and Ludgate Circus in the hub of London's newspaper world, surrounded by parking meters, but in the square itself the old residences of the Chinnerys and Dr Johnson have been replaced by modern buildings.

Chinnery's family apparently had Anglo-Irish links though the direct association with the Irish Chinnerys has not been established. Originally from East Anglia, a family by that name branched to Ireland in about 1620 and there divided, one remaining in Ireland and the other moving back to England some 20 years later, shortly before or during the civil war between King Charles 1 and Parliament.

The link between George Chinnery and this family of returned migrants is presumed rather than verified and we take up the family's history again in London with George Chinnery's grandfather, the writing master.

His skill as a writer and a shorthand expert and his residence in Gough Square would have placed him usefully close to possible employers such as the law courts, Lincoln's Inn, The Temple, and the newspapers. He survived until 1791 and saw all his grandchildren born and brought up.

The family had a long link with St Bride's Church in Fleet Street, a short distance from Gough Square. It was here that George Chinnery was baptised and it was there after his death at the age of 84, that Grandfather William was buried. In 1803 his son William, the Madras merchant, was also interred there.

St Bride's Church is not quite the same today as in Chinnery's days. Heavily damaged during World War II it has since been restored though many of the original exterior walls have been retained, as well as its delightfully fanciful five-tiered spire – one of Wren's most beautiful minor churches, though it is overshadowed today by surrounding buildings.

Born and brought up in such a stimulating and creative environment it is hardly surprising that young George Chinnery veered towards the arts. He clearly showed a precocious flair for painting for he entered the Royal Academy Schools in 1792, though a year earlier he had painted his first portrait which was exhibited at the Royal Academy. He was at the time only 17. The following year he showed two portraits and in 1793 three, including a self-portrait, the first of many he was to paint during his life-time. In 1794 when he was 20 he submitted 12 portraits and two more in the following year.

One of his tutors was the great Sir Joshua Reynolds, the most famous portrait painter of his day and first President of the Royal Academy. Reynolds is thought to have made a strong impression on young Chinnery who, like his teacher, drew his inspiration from the old masters but added to it with his own inventiveness.

It was in his 20th year that he earned the following tribute from a contemporary critic: "among the budding candidates for fame this rising young artist is the most prominent. His progress has been rapid almost beyond example and he has rather adopted a new style of painting, somewhat after the manner of Cosway."[4]

Cosway was perhaps the most accomplished of the 18th century miniaturists and painted the chief members of the Prince Regent's court. Chinnery not only painted portraits and occasional landscapes but developed an aptitude for miniatures, several of which survive, and indeed Chinnery described himself as a miniature painter when he moved to Ireland in 1795. Why he went is not certain. Some writers[5] say he may have been related to the prominent Irish politician, Sir Broderick Chinnery, whose portrait he painted. Others[6] suggest that George's father knew Lord Macartney, a former Governor of Madras, and at that time an influential Irishman who in 1795 had undertaken an unsuccessful mission to Peking to set up an Embassy there (not helped incidentally by his refusal to perform the traditional kowtow or act of obeisance to Emperor Chien Lung).

But whatever the connection between William Chinnery and Lord Macartney there is no truth in the suggestion[7] that George Chinnery accompanied him to China.

The decision to leave London and go to Ireland, however, has puzzled many writers in view of the bright future ahead of the young artist and the highly flattering reviews of his work. One writer[8] speculates whether it was the lure of money and good commissions or the wealthy patronage of Sir Broderick Chinnery but whatever the reason he crossed the Irish Sea from Bristol in 1795 and settled in Dublin. He lodged there with a family called Vigne at 27 College Green. James Vigne was a jeweller and two researchers[9] believe that there was a long-standing acquaintance between the Vigne and Chinnery families.

Clearly young George found Dublin a stimulating city. He was given a number of commissions and during the next few years he was to paint several of Dublin's notable citizens as well as members of the Vigne family. Once again, however, critics noted a characteristic that drew comment on occasions later in his life. "The manner of this painter possesses a peculiarity which would enable one anywhere to distinguish his works. They have expression of original genius, bold, but always either palpably unfinished or with as little as possible. It appears to be his wish to paint everything in an uncommon manner, and, of course, to attract the attention which would otherwise be directed to more finished productions of the common walk."[10]

While he soon became highly regarded as a miniaturist and portraitist he was not, as is frequently claimed to this day, ever a member of the Royal Hibernian Academy. The RHA was not incorporated until 1823, 21 years after Chinnery had left for India and it was improbable that he became an absentee member.[11] Unfortunately no records survive.

In Dublin he came into contact with the work of the miniaturist, John Comerford and both men seemed to have derived some stimulus from their association. Comerford was four years older than Chinnery but it was thought to be Chinnery's example and encouragement which induced the older man to abandon large paintings for miniatures and small portrait drawings. In this sphere, Comerford became the most notable of the later Irish-born artists and the rest of his career in Dublin was a success.[12]

Among George Chinnery's paintings in Ireland were portraits of Sir Broderick Chinnery's family, and Mrs Eustace, the old mother-in-law of James Vigne with whom he lodged. Another was General Vallancey "that fertile author of theories most of them baseless but paraded with a great display of erudition."[13] An even more interesting portrait is the Romney-like painting of Marianne Vigne, the second daughter of the jeweller, for it was Marianne whom George Chinnery married when he was 25 years old in 1799. Although Chinnery has shaded the upper part of her face, she seems an attractive woman with slender arms and long graceful fingers. It is worth keeping this picture of Marianne in mind for in later years Chinnery was to denounce her as the "ugliest woman I have ever seen" — not once but many times — and to name her as one of the chief causes of his flight from India to Macau.

It is not certain at what stage of his marriage Chinnery formed this opinion. In the first two years, he fathered two children, Matilda and John in 1800-1801, and this period of their life seems to have been one of connubial bliss. During this time he also made his mark on Dublin's art world.

Other portraits he painted were of Maria Vigne, his sister in law, Michael Caven, a brother-in-law who married another of the Vigne girls; Ann, Countess of Mornington, Minian Mahaffey and Mr Cooke, a celebrated musician at the Theatre Royal. He also painted miniatures of other theatrical personalities of Dublin, some of which were subsequently engraved, including those of Signor Bianchi, John Philip Kemble and William Lewis.

Under the aegis of General Vallancey, who was reputed to be a powerful figure in the Royal Dublin Society, he became a member of a special committee charged with supervising life classes. Chinnery was, however, a man of restless energies and unsettled habits and his output in Ireland included not just remarkable portraits but attractive landscapes and noteworthy miniatures. He also showed a keen interest in sketching which was later to develop into a massive outpouring of impressions of life in India and China.

But if Chinnery's portraits drew favourable comments at times he also attracted his share of criticism, one describing a picture he submitted to the Royal Dublin Society in 1801 called

Attention in these terms: "It is a picture in which the most difficult attitudes and the greatest variety of drapery have, like the motley penmanship of a Christmas piece, been assembled to display the powers of the artist who wishes to appear to paint everything in an uncommon manner".[14] The portrait of Mr Cooke was described as "an excellent likeness but coarsely executed." As for his landscapes, the critic took him to task for "the stripes of scarlet, black, purple and yellow" which appeared in his picture called *Sunset in Killarney*. In more recent times, however, a writer has come to Chinnery's rescue by saying that his anonymous critic may never have seen Killarney on a July evening when the sun shines out after rain and "colours show on the hill and in the sky that are well nigh incredible to any but those fortunate enough to catch a glimpse of them".[15]

Among his early paintings some were purchased by the Royal Dublin Society following a recommendation he made to the Society to set up a special fund to buy notable paintings as an incentive to young artists. Another achievement was to revive the dormant Society of Artists in Ireland. As Secretary of a new and enthusiastic committee Chinnery put it on its feet and organised exhibitions of Irish paintings.[16]

So great was his impact on the world of Irish art that in 1801, shortly before he left for London, he was presented with a silver palette by the artists of Dublin. It is inscribed: "In testimony of his exertion in promoting the Fine Arts in Ireland, this palette was presented to Mr Geo. Chinnery by the Artists of Dublin, July 27, 1801." [17]

Some indication of the artist's output during his relatively brief stay in Ireland can be realised from the 12 pictures he submitted to the exhibition of the Society of Artists in 1800, eight of which were portraits in oil and three in crayons.[18] There was also a large subject picture entitled *Satan's arrival on the confines of Light*.

The following year he contributed 11 portraits and landscapes to the exhibition held in Parliament House in Dublin. One biographer says his capacity for work and rapidity of execution was phenomenal, and his choice of subjects was as diversified as the mediums he used. He painted in oil and water colour with equal success, drew in pencil and Indian ink and was successful in miniature and pastel portraiture. "His portraits often masquerade as Romneys, Raeburns or Hoppners." [19]

Whether it was the hectic pace of life in Ireland or whether he found he had made a mistake in tying himself down to a wife and children is not known but he became restless and some writers suggest he also began running into debt though there is no proof of this. The authors of one book on Chinnery [20] claim that his spendthrift ways developed during these years but research has failed to support this view. The Dictionary of National Biography suggested that perhaps another reason for his departure was his alleged complicity in the 1798 rebellion. But this has not been substantiated. The revolution, influenced as it was by events in France, was quickly put down, yet Chinnery stayed on in Ireland until 1802, more than a year after the Act of Union with England. It is, moreover, difficult to recall finding a single political statement in surviving letters or shorthand notes.

As for incipient marital difficulties, one writer [21] has said that Chinnery would have been a difficult husband for any wife to manage, what with his emotional weaknesses and innate bohemianism and he suggests that the parting of the none too substantial ties began at about this time. Once again, however, recent research has failed to produce any evidence of trouble between them before Chinnery left for India. [22]

A more pressing reason for his decision is thought to have been money. Having married at the age of 25 and with two young children to support he was too young to make much money in his profession which was then poorly paid.[23] When he found he was not going to make his fortune in Ireland he was impressed by the flock of painters who went to India – men like Zoffany and the two Daniells – and found it something of a Klondike.

There is another reason offered by a critic.[24] Travel was considered to be an occupational necessity of the early English water-colourists and from a purely artistic point of view the Orient held a special fascination for artists. Many who had toured England and Wales and then made the Grand Tour of Europe found India a "sumptuous extension and the romantic spirit was excited by its exotic promise and the novelties of a picturesque country not yet explored." It was not surprising that Thomas Daniell who had previously roamed the English counties at the age of 35 should set sail for the East, a year after Zoffany, taking with him his young nephew, William. No less surprising was it, therefore, that Chinnery should follow, particularly as he had connections with the country through his father's interest in the firm of Chase, Sewell and Chinnery in Madras.

If this helps to explain Chinnery's reasons for leaving Ireland, and a few months later London, why did he leave behind a young wife with two young children? The East India Company was averse to giving a passage to India on its ships to anyone except naval and civil officers of the service, and also supercargoes.[25] The Company tried to discourage people who took advantage of joining them, getting a passage and then leaving to work on their own and the rule was that no wives could accompany their husbands unless they could put up a substantial security.

Chinnery on his first application to the Company was refused a passage to India and while waiting he set up a studio at 20 Lower Brook Street, Grosvenor Square, obviously anticipating a long delay, and exhibited portraits of his brother's children in the Royal Academy that year. These were the three children of William Bassett Chinnery, a Clerk in the Treasury, who had risen rapidly in the Civil Service. He had become Agent General for the Bahamas in 1794, then for New South Wales and other colonies and these posts had brought him in an income of more than £4,000 a year. William established his residence at Gilwell Hall, Essex, and there launched into an expensive way of life. He bought *objets d'art* and gave costly concerts. Although criticised for his extravagance, and indeed the subject of a Treasury inquiry, he continued to spend freely. In 1812, two years after the first inquiry, another was launched and this time he was exposed. His investigator wrote "He deceived me most terribly in 1810 and he is in arrear even beyond your conception. I have directed him to be removed from his situation at the Treasury and all his agencies." Chinnery was found to be in default to the extent of £81,000. He escaped to Gothenburg and died in Paris in 1834. All Chinnery's property, his collection of statuary, vases and pictures were sold, and proceedings lasted 10 years until 1822.[26]

This brief diversion is interesting for a number of reasons. It provides an intriguing parallel between the life style of William Bassett Chinnery and, as we shall see, George Chinnery during his years in Calcutta. While one would hesitate to describe this as a family trait, both brothers evinced a marked lack of financial responsibility which was to end in the downfall of one and the hasty departure from Calcutta to Macau of the other. A second point of interest, however, is that William Bassett Chinnery's home, Gilwell Hall, is where George Chinnery's wife, Marianne, is said to have stayed after her husband's departure.[27] A third point is that the ship on which George Chinnery finally sailed to India was named the *Gilwell*. Whether it was in some way connected with the family's business in

Madras, has never been established though one respected researcher[28] believes it was mere coincidence.

It is worth adding that besides his father's connection with Madras, George Chinnery's brother, John Terry Chinnery, born four years earlier, went out to India in 1792 on the recommendation of one of the Directors of the East India Company, Simon Frazer, and took up the post of Assistant under the Secretary in the Political and Military Department in Madras from August 1 of that year. The following year he became Assistant under the Resident at Cuddalore and in March, 1810 he became a partner in the agency house of Chase, Sewell and Chinnery which by the end of that year had changed its name to Chase, Chinnery and Macdowell. In 1812 he became Commissioner Resident Northern Division. He died in Madras in 1817. Another member of George Chinnery's family also went to India. George's sister, Frances Hughes, three years his junior, embarked in 1796. She travelled on the same ship as a Miss Payton who was on her way to marry John Chinnery. Frances was going to India to marry John Duncan of the East India Company's medical service, the marriage taking place on April 27, 1797. Duncan died in April, 1819.[29]

Chinnery thus had more than casual connections with Madras and this seemed a logical starting point for the young artist. In leaving his wife he nevertheless sent her regular remittances. It was to be another 16 years before the family was reunited. It did not take long for Chinnery once in India to succumb to the gold lust and he was in no hurry to saddle himself with the family. The break with Ireland and England marked a watershed in his life. In deciding to leave, he effectively cut himself off from his many outstanding contemporaries with whom he had studied during his teens in the Royal Academy, as well as the artistic influences that were flowering in England at the time and were to produce such great men as Constable, Girtin, Hoppner, Turner and Lawrence, after the great age of Gainsborough, Reynolds, Wilson and Romney.

It has often been asked whether Chinnery's stature would have risen higher had he remained in England. But before answering this question we must follow Chinnery to India and examine his life and work there which led to his final move to Macau where he spent the last 27 years of his life.

2

An early masterpiece

THE departure of a fleet of ships for India in the early 19th century was an impressive sight. A historian has described the great sight of "20 or more three-masters in double line passing down the Channel, protected by watchful frigates of the Royal Navy busily flagging signals." [1]

On board, life was invariably an ordeal and the men who went down to the sea in ships in those days were a spartan breed. In Chinnery's case, the ship he travelled on was only two years old. She had a single deck and displaced 400 tons. Like most East India Company ships she was privately owned – in this case by a firm called Law and Co – and rented out for the voyage. She was commanded by Captain G. Sheen and her home port was London. [2]

From June 11, 1802 Chinnery was at sea for six months, a not unusual experience. He appears to have been singularly inactive during this time although he was later a keen student of the craft which sailed the quiet waters of the Hooghly River in India and the Pearl River estuary in China.

With all this time at his disposal it might have been supposed that Chinnery would have spent his hours sketching shipboard scenes, his fellow passengers, crew or ports of call, yet there is nothing that can be identified with this or any other period he was at sea. The *Gilwell* of course took the Atlantic route round the Cape of Good Hope and then headed north-east up the Indian Ocean for Madras. Many passengers found the old Atlantic passage "an exceedingly unpleasant experience. Living conditions were cramped, the ships verminous, and food supplies dependent to some extent on calls at St Helena and the Cape not being delayed by bad weather." [3]

Perhaps Chinnery was a poor sailor and was seasick much of the time, though with his East India Company connections he should have enjoyed comfortable quarters. Whatever the reason for his inactivity, he arrived in Madras on December 21, where his brother John was staying.

Dominating the port city was Fort St George which the East India Company had built soon after Francis Day, one of its representatives in southern India, had obtained a grant of land from the local ruler. The fort became a massively protected trading post and inevitably around its walls flourished camp followers; this evolved into a settlement which was to become the third city of India boasting a population of 2.5 million people. It was the first land acquired by the East India Company on the sub-continent and in 1658 became headquarters for its Indian establishments.

Chinnery has left us a sketch of the Fort surmounted by a massive Union Jack fluttering from a flag pole, with the native catamarans and Massoolah boats drawn up on the beach in

This painting is signed above the right shoulder of the lady "G.C.E.I. 1803". This miniature on ivory measures 3 ins by 2½ ins and was painted in Madras, the year after the artist's arrival in India.

This miniature on ivory (6 by 5 ins) is fully signed, dated and inscribed on the back in Chinnery's own handwriting: "Geo Chinnery Madras Pinxit 1803 – to be kept from damp and sun". The painting shows two ladies, one seated wearing a white dress with a black lace shawl and a light blue kerchief covering her hair and the other standing and wearing a dress of royal blue. It was painted the year after Chinnery arrived in India.

the foreground. Although the water-line has receded since Chinnery's time the boats can still be seen on the beach and Fort St George remains an impressive landmark.

That first Christmas and New Year was important for the young artist who met many of the city's leading figures, but although several signed miniatures survive, all dated 1803, in the East India Registers he is entered among the European residents as "out of employ" in the following year. In 1805 and 1806 however he is listed as a portrait painter. Chinnery found people in Madras not very different from those in London, Dublin or any other major city in the kind of picture they wanted him to paint. As one art critic has written of the portraits of that era: "they looked pretty much the same in Cawnpore as in Chiswick and were expected to be portrayed in the established manner of Reynolds or Romney." In Chinnery's case the miniature at which he excelled was almost as highly prized as the portrait though he was also to find very quickly that the lucrative commissions were the full length official portraits of leading administrators, judges, generals and Indian nabobs, often publicly subscribed and generally destined for a place of honour in some palace, court, or stately residence.

One of his Madras portraits was of the distinguished civil servant, Peter Cherry,[4] but perhaps Chinnery's best known painting of this period, was of William and Catharine Aurora, the Eurasian children of Colonel James Achilles Kirkpatrick by his wife Khair-un-Nissa Begum, niece of the Prime Minister of Hyderabad. This is an outstanding work which hangs in the board room of the Hongkong and Shanghai Banking Corporation in Hongkong, next to the equally imposing portrait of their father.

The painting of the children is remarkable as much for its size (61 x 46½ ins) as for its high quality, and many years later was to bring tears of nostalgia to an older Catharine who rediscovered it hanging in the home of the former Chief Justice of Bengal, Sir Henry Russell, in Reading.

It is noteworthy for another characteristic and that is the lavish use of vermilion which Chinnery was to employ increasingly in his paintings to highlight special features. In the painting, the heads of the two children seem disproportionately large and a prominent physician on seeing it in Hongkong speculated that they might have been suffering from rickets, a vitamin D deficiency disease common at that time among young children in India.

The date of the painting is not certain but a historian[5] believes it must have been painted before 1805, as on September 10 of that year, the two children were sent to England on board the *Lord Hawkesbury*, with Capt George Elers as a fellow passenger. In his memoirs he writes: "We had on board a Mrs Ure, wife of a Dr Ure of Hyderabad, who had two fine children of three and four years old under her charge, the children of Colonel James Achilles Kirkpatrick, by a Princess, to whom report says he was married. Her Highness would not part with her children until £10,000 had been settled on each of them. They were a boy and a girl, and they had a faithful old black man who was very fond of them to attend upon them." The vessel arrived in Portsmouth on February 15, 1806 and the two children were duly handed over to the care of their uncle, Colonel William Kirkpatrick, two days later.

Why the children were sent away from India is not known but the girl in the picture, Catharine, grew up to be a great beauty and was the "Kitty" of Carlyle's essay *Reminiscences* and the "Blumine" of his *Sartor Resartus*. She married Captain James Winsloe Phillips of the 7th Hussars and died on March 2, 1889 at Torquay. Her brother died earlier leaving a widow and three children.[6]

Chinnery painted this portrait when he was about 30 years old and was said to have been paid a large fee for it. It was one of his early masterpieces which helped to establish his reputation as one of the most gifted portrait painters to live in India. It has not been possible to establish a chronological record of his works following this. Various historians have at one time or another attributed paintings to Chinnery which on closer investigation have turned out to be the works of other less gifted artists and because of his neglect or reluctance to sign and date his pictures it is difficult to establish how many he painted in this or indeed any other period. Some, moreover, which he is thought to have painted, have not been seen for many years.

Chinnery signed some of his miniatures. One, in the possession of the Hongkong and Shanghai Banking Corporation, from his Madras period is signed above the right shoulder of the lady "G.C. E.I. 1803," while another miniature on ivory is inscribed on the back in his own handwriting "Geo. Chinnery, Madras, Pinxit 1803" with the added advice "To be kept from Damp and Sun."

One portrait which does bear a signature is that of Lady Grant, a gouache now in the possession of the Hongkong and Shanghai Banking Corporation, though experts[7] question whether it is Chinnery's work. The painting is a triple enigma for not only is its authenticity doubted despite its prominent "G. Chinnery" signature, but its date is uncertain as indeed is the identity of Lady Grant. An expert[8] has pointed out that the signature differs from others which are considered to be genuine, and while the Bank's own catalogue places it in the Indian period, others[9] believe it was painted prior to India. What adds strength to this belief is that while there were several Grants in India (and others in Macau) the nearest titled Grant appears to be Sir Patrick, C-in-C Madras and later C-in-C India but this was not until the Indian mutiny in 1857, five years after Chinnery's death and 32 years after he left India. As for the Macau Grants whom Chinnery sketched in 1837, there was no title in the family. The wife, a French lady, played a guitar and this is shown in the foreground of the charming family portrait that Chinnery submitted to the Royal Academy. The husband was a sea Captain who commanded an opium hulk at Whampoa. The portrait of Lady Grant, however, remains a mystery.

One of the greatest disservices done to Chinnery has been the attribution of paintings to him by sales rooms and fine art dealers with fragmentary knowledge of his life and works and seemingly little desire to establish the truth. One book suggested that in 1805 and 1806 Chinnery went to Ceylon and attributed to him watercolours painted at about that time.[10] These however have turned out to be the work of other artists.

In 1807, however, we pick up the Chinnery story again with the publication of a new monthly journal called Indian Magazine and European Miscellany of which Chinnery was described as the joint proprietor.[11] The magazine appeared in February of that year and continued until April, 1808 when it seems to have come to a sudden end. This was 10 months after Chinnery left Madras to visit Calcutta though whether his departure was responsible for its ceasing publication we do not know.

Later that year an extract was published entitled *Views in Madras* and a copy was subsequently found in the Imperial Library at Calcutta.[12] The booklet contains seven pictures, six of which are by Chinnery and are signed "Geo: Chinnery delt et aqua f. 1807." The seventh was by J. Gantz, a well-known local artist.

These show a *View of the Banqueting Room and Part of Government House, Madras,* and *North east view of Fort St George.* Two others are of native boats, one being of catamarans and the other Massoolah boats, these latter vessels consisting of planks literally stitched together with coir rope with enough slack in the stitching to enable them to hold together despite the heaviest pounding in the surf. The steersman stood in the stern using an oar as the rudder and one writer has observed that "the dexterity with which he balances in the heavy seas is perfectly astonishing." [13]

Another mention of Chinnery occurs on January 28, 1807 [14] where a description is given of an entertainment at the Pantheon on January 22 to celebrate the acquittal of Lord Melville, a former Commissioner of the Board of Control of Indian Affairs and later First Lord of the Admiralty in 1804-5 and widely respected as a shrewd Scottish politician which in turn earned him the nickname of "King Harry the Ninth." Suspicions of his financial management at the Admiralty, however, led to his impeachment for corruption in 1806 but this ended in acquittal. The decorations at the Pantheon included a large transparency painted by Chinnery representing Justice unveiling Truth to Britannia. Each guest was presented with an etching by Chinnery, depicting Lord Melville's action in providing for the widows and orphans of the seamen killed in the war against France and Spain, culminating in the Battle of Trafalgar. [15]

While he had completed a number of highly regarded paintings and presumably received good fees for them, there are suggestions that he also developed a taste for extravagant living and began running up big bills, finally becoming involved with Indian moneylenders. He was also at this time sending remittances to his wife in England but while there is no reason to doubt that Chinnery met his family obligations at this time the evidence of extravagance is mainly hearsay.

The year 1807 was however a milestone in Chinnery's life. He was invited to Calcutta to paint the portrait of the Chief Justice of the Supreme Court of Bengal, Sir Henry Russell, and such a commission could only have come as a result of the high reputation he gained as a portraitist in Madras. He travelled north on a vessel named the *City of London*, leaving Madras on June 20, on the 1,000 mile journey up the Coromandel coast to British India's second great city. Calcutta, dominated by Fort William, had come under East India Company control when Job Charnock secured its lease for an annual rent of 1,200 rupees in 1698.

Chinnery set about his task early in July. William Hickey was then living in the city and wrote in his diaries of his meetings with the artist. Hickey recalls that "the principal natives of the settlement had, by an elegant address in the Persian language, entreated Sir Henry to sit for the portrait" with the intention of exhibiting it in the Town Hall.

Russell received Chinnery with every courtesy and, so Hickey tells us, "allotted to his exclusive use two handsome apartments, and of course considered him one of the family, a cover always being laid for him at the dinner table." According to the diarist Chinnery first drew several sketches of the bewigged judge (as was his custom in portraits). He consulted Hickey about these, "appearing himself partial to the one he carried into effect, which as it likewise happened to please me above all the rest was particularly gratifying to him."

Chinnery set to work in the Court room as it was the middle of the vacation and Hickey tells us he spent two or three hours a day watching his progress. "He laboured incessantly, being generally at work from sunrise until sunset; it took him near three months ere the picture was completed, he being twice obliged to lay it by for several days on account of severe indisposition." He completed it by September, 1807, when the Persian Ambassador paid Russell a visit and much admired the portrait.

According to the Government Gazette: "This production is one of the finest specimens of Mr Chinnery's talents, which are universally acknowledged to be rare and splendid."

He pictured the judge lounging in an arm chair; by his feet lay the sword of justice and the

One of Chinnery's early official portraits which brought him fame in India. The above picture shows Sir Henry Russell, Chief Justice of the Supreme Court of Bengal, painted in 1807, as it hangs today in the High Court in Calcutta. The mace and sword are shown in the engraved version, in the picture opposite.

— Courtesy Registrar of the High Court, Calcutta.

12

mace of authority.   In the background, the blindfolded figure of Justice, holding the scales in her right hand, leans on a pillar protecting a child representing innocence.   It is a splendid portrait, and Hickey was fair in his praise of it when it was finished.   He described it as "a picture (which) did Mr Chinnery infinite credit as an artist and must prove his genius so long as a particle of the canvas remains."

Shortly after, Chinnery painted a portrait of Hickey who described it as "a very capital likeness" and this was presented to Sir Henry Russell and hung in his dining room in the court house in Calcutta.

Having completed the portrait of Russell,   Chinnery then suggested an engraving be made provided there were 200 subscribers willing to take copies.   Hickey claims that he personally obtained the names of 107 subscribers from whom he collected three gold mohurs each "which I forthwith handed to Mr Chinnery who in consequence thereof directly commenced a small copy of the original work from which the engraving was to be executed and which I was to take charge of and convey to the engraver in England."   However, before the work had been completed, poor Chinnery went down with severe inflammation of the eyes which incapacitated him completely.   Hickey adds: "During the remainder of my stay in Bengal he was obliged to shut himself up, excluding almost every ray of light from his bedchamber, his spirits being so depressed he would not admit Sir Henry Russell or any friend whomsoever in which melancholy state I left him."

Hickey adds that following his departure from Calcutta he heard that Chinnery "became determinedly insane and has ever since been kept under restriction, being now pronounced a confirmed and incurable lunatic."   Where Hickey heard this story is not known.   Chinnery recovered from his affliction and completed the painting for the engraving which was undertaken by S. W. Reynolds in London and duly appeared as a reproduction on the frontispiece to Hickey's fourth volume.   It is true, however, that Chinnery experienced extremes of depression and melancholia while at other times he was gay, carefree, chatty and excellent company.

The effect that Chinnery's portrait of Russell had upon the Calcutta establishment was clearly sensational.   Although as many as 60 British and European painters had visited India in preceding years, to most people the Russell masterpiece stamped him as one of the greatest, as well as a most sensitive portraitist.

A flood of commissions followed with the promise of rich takings and Chinnery could virtually pick and choose his clients from among the top people.   Additionally he was lionised by society and was invited by many a hostess to sit among the select of the land in punkah-cooled dining rooms lavishly furnished with the finest of silverware and the best fare in Calcutta.   This was heady stuff for Chinnery.

It is estimated [16] that at the height of his fame in Calcutta, his income was £500 a month and if true this was an incredibly high figure.   Contemporary scholars, such as Mr Richard Ormond of the National Portrait Gallery in London, do not believe he ever earned so much.   But while his actual income is a matter of conjecture, Chinnery became improvident, capricious and careless about money. [17]   There is less dispute about this.

British art dealers have helped to foster the legend of Chinnery as a dashing man about town by ascribing to him pictures he never painted and accomplishments he never performed.   These have been reproduced in contemporary volumes [18] and show tiger hunt scenes which Chinnery is alleged to have painted.   Modern critics however dismiss these as the work of an inferior painter, though one is reported to have on its back a label which says "The

14

four sporting pictures of tiger-shooting and pig sticking were painted by Chinnery; painter to the King of Oudh, 1820-1825; for Robert Castle Jenkins – the artist himself on horseback."[19]

It is doubtful whether Chinnery ever held such a post because he was not in that part of the country, or if so for a short period which has passed unrecorded. However the last reference to Chinnery on horseback calls for comment. A sketch by Chinnery has been found showing two men on galloping horses, apparently wielding 'pig sticks'. Both riders appear to be turbanned Indians, one with a beard. However the tiger hunt oils bear little resemblance to his style. Moreover the impression one has of Chinnery is that he would have been the last person to take part in a tiger hunt, much less ride horseback and stick pigs with a lance – though no doubt he would have enjoyed dining out on such an escapade.

Chinnery was a notorious story-teller and probably had paranoiac tendencies. He told W. C. Hunter, his close friend in Macau years later[20] a story about his "first experience in natural history" during his time in India. It seems to be apocryphal but quite apart from its credibility it provides an illuminating insight into Chinnery's nature. And as it falls in his India period it is best told here.

Hunter recalls that Chinnery was having dinner in a bungalow in India and was sitting at the opposite end of the table to his host. Towards the end of dinner, Chinnery became aware of a snake "making acquaintance with my ankle by twisting itself about it." Noiselessly and unseen it had glided in from the verandah. Chinnery ordered everyone to be quiet and "in a voice scarcely above his breath, directed a servant to bring him a bowl of milk and a cane; his manner and look assuring silence, he deliberately placed the former on the floor a short distance from his chair and as quietly lowered the cane close to it, while still holding the handle. The odour of the milk attracted the snake, which immediately uncoiled itself from the ankle on (to) the stick. In another moment while in the enjoyment of its unlooked for feed he sprang from the chair, jumped on the bowl and on the head of the uninvited guest, destroying it and its dinner in the twinkling of an eye."

This is a typical Chinnery story and no doubt added much to his popularity as a guest who helped to liven any dinner party. It cannot be doubted that Chinnery had at one time seen or heard of someone killing a snake in this way, but whether he would have had the presence of mind to have accomplished such a feat, much less the athletic prowess to have taken part in a vigorous chase after wild boar, remains shrouded in doubt.

Let us not confuse the artist with the legendary figure that many writers make him out to be. He was no superman and indeed his own self-portraits from the India period show him to be a somewhat plump, studious, bespectacled figure, with a shock of hair, soft full lips, craggy eye-brows, fleshy nose and deep-set eyes. There is intellectual depth in that face, humour and sensitivity in those eyes, but not the masculine vigour one would expect of a sporting gentleman born to the saddle.

However, in his earlier years, Chinnery must have been a keen walker and he was a devoted student of the Indian countryside with a genuine love for it. Although he earned his living by painting portraits, his real life was the countryside. He filled notebook after notebook with village scenes. He showed tumbledown mud huts with their peculiar thatched roofs, and villages with their stony, muddy paths strewn with broken pots. He sketched bullocks grazing by the wayside, chickens scratching at the ground and villagers carrying waterpots on their heads with a dignity that would have done credit to a maharajah.

In 1808, a year after arriving in Calcutta, Chinnery left for Dacca in south-east Bengal and this, and his final hectic period in Calcutta, forms the subject of the next few chapters.

These two engravings were made from sketches by George Chinnery and published in India in 1807 and show (above) a view of the banqueting room and part of Government House, Madras, and Massoolah boats drawn up on the beach outside Madras.

3

Chinnery and D'Oyly

HISTORIANS have often alleged impecuniosity, wife trouble or Chinnery's erratic nature to explain his sudden moves but the Dacca interlude could not have been prompted by any of these. It would have required spending on a massive scale to have landed him in financial difficulties so quickly although there is little doubt he got through a good deal of his money at this time. Perhaps the main reason for going was the offer of lucrative commissions, for among his paintings in Dacca were those of a number of Indian notables, including the Nawabs.

At first Indians were unwilling to sit for Chinnery because of a superstition that it would bring on premature death. However Babu Gopi Mohun Tagore consented to sit for Chinnery as did his sons Nanda Kumar and Kali Kumar.[1] Another to be painted was the Nawab Sadat Ali Khan and his brother, portraits which brought commendations from several British visitors to the Nawab's home in Dacca. In turn these helped bring further commissions for Chinnery, both from Indian notables and British administrators. We are told that he worked on these portraits for several months "under most congenial conditions, without pressures, either domestic or financial".[2]

It was not just the lucrative commissions that attracted Chinnery, however. It was in Dacca that Chinnery drew many of his Bengal sketches, filling a series of notebooks with pencil jottings of landscapes, temples and mosques, villagers and animals, some of which were later filled in with pen and ink. There was usually a decorative frontispiece, often in the form of a landscape with the year and the subject, for example *Sketches in Bengal* inscribed on a piece of fallen stonework or plinth. It has been suggested[3] that this was probably the only way Chinnery was able to achieve some order in his prolific output, though others believe that Chinnery envisaged eventual publication.[4] He made the same sort of sketches in Macau apparently to provide friends and customers with treasured souvenirs.

Another reason why Chinnery found the Dacca interlude so refreshing and stimulating was that he was among a group of talented amateur artists drawn from civil and military circles and this may also help to account for the length of time he spent in the city and the relative serenity and peace of mind he found there.

He also struck up a friendship which was to last for many years in Dacca and later Calcutta. This was with Sir Charles D'Oyly who had been posted there as Collector and from their association an important influence was created for artists in India, both native and expatriate. For D'Oyly himself was an amateur artist and writer and took lessons from Chinnery.[5] He later referred to Chinnery as "the ablest limner in the land"

and one only has to look at D'Oyly's pen-and-ink sketches to see his strong influence.

Chinnery imparted much more than his own techniques, his vision and a love of sketching, however. D'Oyly initiated an art society in 1824 in Behar not just to encourage art among like-minded people but "also for the circulation of fun and merriment of all descriptions".[6] And to this were invited residents of Patna, Bankipur and outlying districts. Under D'Oyly's leadership, cheerful groups set off on sketching expeditions on horseback and D'Oyly has left us sketches of these outings, with the men in top hats and riding boots and women wearing bonnets and gowns with leg-of-mutton sleeves.[7]

The D'Oylys were, like Chinnery, somewhat unconventional people in this rather strait-laced society and were popular and respected wherever they went. Chinnery's portrait of Sir Charles and Lady D'Oyly shows them in fancy dress, and they were then young, good-humoured, self-assured people. Incidentally this was D'Oyly's second wife, Elizabeth, his first wife, Marion, who was also his cousin, having died a few years earlier. It was almost certainly the first wife whom Chinnery knew in Dacca.

To Chinnery, the D'Oylys seemed kindred spirits and together they took part in amateur theatricals, a popular pastime among the expatriate community. But enjoyable as this association was, D'Oyly was keen to share his experience with others. They not only attracted expatriate artists to their circle but Indians from Murshidabad in Bengal who had come to Dacca to paint pictures for the British community. The D'Oylys invited a number of these artists to their home, showed them books of European prints and encouraged them to paint in a style more acceptable to British tastes.[8] D'Oyly also bought pictures from them to send to his friends. One artist named Jairam Das, was trained to work his lithographic press which he had ordered from Britain to publish the pictures drawn by members of his society, and within a short time Patna gained the reputation of being "the most cultivated station" in Upper India. Chinnery's influence was indirect but nevertheless important in the encouragement he showed D'Oyly who in turn imparted it to his fellow expatriates and to Indian artists.

Chinnery stayed in Dacca for a period of four years before moving to Calcutta where he opened a studio and he was to live there for 10 years. With his reputation as a talented portraitist established, he set in train a process of high living which was to bring about his eventual bankruptcy and which no doubt contributed to his final separation from his wife.

It appears that very soon after he returned to Calcutta he took an Indian mistress by whom he had two sons about a year later. Her identity is not known. It would seem that the children were twins and their year of birth is deduced from the fact that both died in the year 1841 and were buried in Calcutta. Strangely only a few months separated their deaths. One — Edward Charles Chinnery — was aged 27 years and three months; the other, Henry Collins Chinnery was 28.

While little is known of their lives, one of the boys — Henry Chinnery — is said to have taken up his father's profession and at least three paintings in Calcutta traditionally associated with Chinnery, are thought to be the work of the son.[9] It is also reported that this same Henry Chinnery was sent to England in 1836 by the Nawab of Murshidabad on a mission to present gifts to King William IV. One of these gifts was a full-length portrait of the Nawab by an artist named W. H. F. Hutchisson. Henry Chinnery sailed for England[10] in a vessel named *Robarts* on March 12, 1836 and we learn that the King received the presents and gave Chinnery in return a gold watch, as well as a number of gifts for the Nawab,[11] including the Insignia of the Order of Guelph. After his return

A buffalo sleeps by its cart outside a villager's hut in India in this ink sketch drawn in 1818, while in the picture below villagers rest with their cattle in a clearing in the Bengal countryside.

These are two of Chinnery's early ink sketches in Dacca, during his visit in
1808. Drawn within two days of one another, these pictures illustrate a
mosque on the bank of a river (above) and a part of the old fort with the
mosque in the background at the Great Cottra.

— Courtesy Victoria and Albert Museum

to Calcutta, Henry Chinnery was employed in the Civil Auditor's Office. He was buried in that city on September 25, 1841. His brother had died on January 14 of the same year. It is said that the brother's record was "unsatisfactory".[12] Some years before he had got into trouble for larceny [13] and was said to be unemployed at the time of his death.

In 1812, however, the liaison with the Indian woman and the subsequent birth of the two boys added more financial burdens to one who was already saddled with the costs of maintaining a young family and a wife in England. At this stage Chinnery appears to have given no thought to bringing them to Calcutta — that was to come four years later. Several important commissions and many minor ones were keeping him busy.

The picture we have of Chinnery in his heyday in Calcutta is mainly of an extrovert personality; he is said to have talked loudly, been very boisterous and was fond of singing during his work.[14] His puns were infamous, sometimes clever but often obscure — D'Oyly described them as "execrable" — though again they demonstrate an intelligent, lively mind and these together with a fund of stories which passed for amusing in those days, made him a popular guest at many of the best homes in India. In an age long before the advent of the telephone, Chinnery was also an avid correspondent. Many letters have survived and are quoted in the course of these chapters. Reference was made earlier to Chinnery's sister, Frances, who married Dr John Duncan in Madras and in a letter to his pupil in Calcutta, Mrs Browne, he reveals that he corresponded with her.

Sir Charles D'Oyly has drawn a cartoon showing Chinnery at work in his studio in Calcutta — and in those days he wore his hair long and kept it in place with a semi-circular tortoise shell comb that had "once graced the swell of crinal horrors that adorned an Indian belle".[15] The cartoon bears out the state of hectic activity in his studio where a mythical newcomer to India, Tom Raw, sits for his portrait by the most famous artist in the city.

Sir Charles provided another revealing insight into Chinnery's life in his doggerel verse entitled *The Studio of George Chinnery*.[16] This tells us that it was situated "up a vile lane whose odour makes one sick". To gain entry one did not bother knocking but walked in kicking the people sleeping on the staircase on the way.

He says that inside his studio:
"Imprimis o'er the walls are charcoal dashings
of sudden thoughts — or imitative keys
hung on a nail — and various coloured splashings —
the shape of frames, of houses, horses, trees,
prismatic circles — five dot effigies,
notes of shorthand — a card for five o'clock
'Lord M desires the honour of Mr C's
company' in conspicuous station stuck
to shew deference paid his talent — or his luck"

Further verses provide a revealing insight into Chinnery's life and work style.
"Close to his window is a drawing table
where, erst, in miniature engaged, he toiled,
and near a chair and hookah, when he's able
to contemplate the canvas he has oiled:
in this enjoyment were he ever foiled,
adieu to talent — 'Tis his next great pleasure

to painting, he has often said (and smiled),
the sitting over, to devote his leisure
in smoky meditation o'er his new wrought treasure.

A teapoy groaning with odd tomes and scraps
of undigested journals, stands behind,
sketch books, surmounted by his flannel caps,
loose prints, and notes — some very far from kind,
with pretty little chits from dames that wind
him round their little finger — lawyers letters dunning
for clients, most solicitous to grind,
and drafts of letter, full of wit and punning
and house accounts that still keep forever running".

In a further stanza, Sir Charles records that Chinnery kept one or two paintings by his former tutor, Sir Joshua Reynolds, in a storeroom and would sit and gaze at them and imagine himself as another Reynolds.[17] D'Oyly's poem has provoked speculation that Chinnery was an opium smoker. The authors of one book[18] feel this conclusion is inescapable and that he may well have acquired the taste before he got to Dacca. They go on to state that indulgence in the drug among the British in India was neither unusual nor considered a vice and they add that Chinnery would have found the delights of withdrawal into a dream of fantasy irresistible. They concluded that the allusion to Chinnery's "smoking" in his studio was explicit although couched in delicate allegory.

This is a controversial viewpoint not shared by all researchers who point out that if recourse to this drug was not considered unusual why D'Oyly should couch his references in allegorical form. As a former Opium Agent in Bechar there was no reason for D'Oyly to refer to the drug in euphemistic terms.

Chinnery was of course surrounded by opium both in India and China and it was not uncommon to find merchants and officials smoking it. Furthermore D'Oyly's reference to "smoky meditation" finds an echo in a manuscript written by Captain Robert Bennet Forbes who recalls that Chinnery left Calcutta partly because his wife, who arrived in 1818, had "become aware of certain peccadillos to which he had become addicted". Once again the "peccadillo" is not described but his use of the word "addicted" suggests it was opium.

Chinnery was indeed known for two indulgences which an old Macau friend[19] recalls in a book written years after Chinnery's death. "During the whole time that Mr Chinnery had passed amongst us, 27 years, he had been remarked for two characteristics one of being an enormous eater, the other of never drinking either wine, beer or spirits. His sole beverage was tea, oftener cold than hot." Again no mention of opium, though he did smoke tobacco and take snuff.

Another point that emerges from the D'Oyly poem is that Chinnery was in regular correspondence with "dames that wind him round their little finger". This is, of course, true and Chinnery's weakness for a pretty face and a neat figure comes through at various times in his life, as was also apparent in his Macau days. Apart from his Indian mistress, however, these were flirtatious encounters which as far as is known never developed into serious affairs. One of these associations, resulted in a prolonged correspondence between the artist and his pupil and it is appropriate to consider this in the next chapter.

This picture of a mosque was sketched in ink in the Indian countryside while the pencil sketch below shows a section of the gate of the old fort at Calcutta, dated Oct 3, 1818.

— Courtesy Victoria and Albert Museum

The frontispiece for Chinnery's sketches of Bengal, undated, and below, the cover for what was possibly another collection of "scraps, poetry and drawings" by Chinnery in 1823.

4

The Mrs Browne affair

ONE of the best documented periods in Chinnery's life is to be found in the collection of letters and fragments of writing which survive from his days in Calcutta and which are now for the most part kept in the British Museum. This was the correspondence between the artist and one of his many pupils, Mrs Maria Browne, spanning a period of ten years (1811-1821) in which Chinnery reveals more about his philosophy and techniques than can be found elsewhere.

Two noted Chinnery scholars have been concerned with the transcription of these letters and the treatise, Mr Richard Ormond, Assistant Keeper of the National Portrait Gallery in London, and Mr Francis B. Lothrop, Hon. Trustee of the Peabody Museum, Salem, Massachusetts. It is possible that more light will be thrown on Chinnery's methods and teachings in the study being made by Mr Geoffrey W. Bonsall, Director of the Hongkong University Press, of Chinnery's extensive shorthand notes which he made especially in Macau and of which a few appear to be a continuation or development of the treatise he began in India.

Chinnery obviously intended at one stage to write a book. In one of his letters to his pupil, Mrs Browne, he said "All these general principles ought to be illustrated by particular examples (like my Book when I write it! is to have each theory, practically illustrated)". As far as we know this book was never completed and while the Calcutta treatise is considered to be only "a sketchy outline of Chinnery's methods and ideas and not a coherent statement"[1] enough survives to enable us to see into the mind of the artist, to follow his approach and technique and to appreciate his qualities as a teacher. They also give us a clearer insight into Chinnery himself for his letters are much more than a series of instructions and corrections to his pupil; he either was, or imagined himself to be in love with her at one time.

Chinnery of course excelled in the company of women and was adept at charming them.[2] In the case of Maria Browne, however, he had the pleasure of teaching one who had attained almost professional standards and he was often fulsome in his praise of her work, though when necessary he was gently but firmly critical of her mistakes and from the surviving correspondence it does not appear that he allowed his feelings to influence his appraisal of her work.

He has been described as "perhaps the most stimulating teacher of drawing who ever went to India"[3] and in his writings on the art of painting and composition we come across someone totally different from the somewhat superficial Chinnery who survives in contemporary accounts. Much has been written about his mercurial temperament, his hypochondria, his eccentricities, his tall stories, his garrulousness, his gross extravagance and inability to manage his own affairs, as well as his relations with his wife and with other women. Yet in his approach to his art, in the execution of his work and in his ability to communicate the finer points to his students we discover a more vital, more acutely perceptive and indeed dedicated person, an artist of intellect and deep understanding, experience and critical power. In his letters to Mrs Browne, Chinnery gave her a mass of advice on the theory and practice of miniature painting — and again some of this is reflected in his shorthand notes in his Macau period.

Mrs Browne was not of course Chinnery's only pupil in India. He taught a number of people in Dacca and again in Calcutta. The works of a number of his more distinguished pupils survive including Sir Charles D'Oyly and John Elliott, a member of the Bengal civil service. However it was Mrs Browne who inspired the letters and who worked with him in preparing the treatise. It should be added that though flirtatious in tone, Chinnery's letters were invariably addressed to "My dear Mrs Browne" and ended with felicitations to her husband whom Chinnery addressed as "Browne". He signed himself "Yours very sincerely, Geo. Chinnery."

His ability to call on them at almost any time of the day, including breakfast, suggests an easy intimacy and though her husband, Marmaduke, a taciturn Captain in the Bengal Artillery, did not share her interest in painting and indeed emerges from contemporary accounts as something of a martinet, there is no hint of hostility or jealousy between them in Chinnery's letters. Mrs Browne, described as "a lively and pretty person" was in her late 20s at the time, and Chinnery was quick to establish a rapport with her. This association was mutually rewarding. Not only were her latent artistic talents to flower under Chinnery's devoted attention but he was persuaded to set out the wealth of technique and experience he had acquired and eventually collate it into a more systematic form.[4] Chinnery showed himself to be well read and there are references to Pope and Dr Johnson. He quotes the Edinburgh Review in criticising Bell's *Anatomy of Expression in Painting* and he gives the impression of being a very thorough, erudite man on all aspects of painting. He quotes from Pope's *Essay on Criticism* that "Men must be taught as if you taught them not; And things unknown propos'd as things forgot". However it is not just his advice that is noteworthy but the way he delivers it. Here is but one sample: "Your sketch is quite admirable — the sentiment, the feeling of it is beautiful! it is arch & very sweet — but still (Oh! If I had you at my Elbow how much I would say — rather how much better I would explain myself than I can with the Shei, Calcum, Cockaye!) the Drawing wants a little — I would almost say don't go on with it till I have the pleasure to see you and I will come any Evening except Tomorrow and Tuesday when I am engaged." In the same letter Chinnery becomes the practical man of art once again. Obviously Mrs Browne has been working on a sketch of Romney's and Chinnery tells her that while the sentiment, feeling and meaning of the picture is perfectly explained, its details are not and "it has been misleading to you — the left Arm of yours is 10 Times as well drawn as his — the right wants improvement and the right hand".

He is ever the tactful and considerate teacher. His letters must have taken up hundreds of hours, yet it is almost certain that he did this as a labour of love, her young and lively company being sufficient recompense. Nowhere in this correspondence is there a suggestion of fees being paid. Yet his financial problems remained a perpetual bugbear for he wrote once in 1817: "If I was not bothered as I am about Finance I would do more, rather I would shew my talent better — now I am shackled — but yet please God all will be well here in Time..." But if domestic worries and a hectic social life often distracted him he was constant in his

26

attentions to his pupil and he derived a considerable amount of pleasure from giving these lessons.

One letter, written in 1813, begins: "And do you think my dear Mrs Browne otherwise than what I wrote this morning was strictly en Badinage? Ha! Ha! Ha! As if I did not understand you yesterday! I only was a little to introduce my Lesson — tho' I paid myself an unnecessary compliment, for I ought to leave it to my friends to find out my little good qualities, for wh you are so obliging to give me credit . . . But besides this, the pupil must never be disheartened, & if too much complaint is made at one time it may dispirit & act quite inversely to what one wishes . . ."

In between the "badinage" and references to his personal problems Chinnery comes through with commentaries such as this one on miniature painting: "The whole as you have put it together is more right than wrong & you have given a very tolerable idea of what I meant in regard to Attitude — but again I must repeat all such parts of the Art are feeling & Idea — this being the Abstract sense of the thing in order to produce Beauty, the thing must be increased — just so when I talk of thickening the Lips and lengthening the Chin — I increase them because no Beauty ever had Thin Lips & a Short Chin!"

In another letter in the same year he tells his pupil of one of her paintings: "The head is now a good shape — the hair is a little too precise & formal — the Ear is a little too small — You see how free I am in my Criticisms but you are aware of my intention & meaning." He then continues with a quotation from his old master, Sir Joshua Reynolds: "Sir Joshua in his admirable & never enough to be admired, Lectures, observes that the Art is full of apparent Contradictions — whether this is the fault of the Art itself, or from the want of Language to express ourselves rightly one can't say — but I imagine it to be the latter; for had our Art not stuck in the mud (excuse this Expression) as it has, & had men who handled the Pencil been on the one hand, Men of Science & Philosophers, or on the other when they were so (& many have been so) liberal men, & given the world their written Art, we might have had a Nomenclature of Terms like other sciences fixed & determined to express ourselves by."

This reference by Chinnery to a "nomenclature of terms" is particularly interesting for it would seem from his shorthand notes found in his sketch books in Macau that he may have been working on some such system. In his treatise which contains advice about miniature and other kinds of oil painting, there is a section on landscape, subdivided into nine stages, which again finds echoes in his shorthand notes. This is discussed in more detail in a later chapter.

Chinnery also enjoyed laying down the law. He wrote dogmatically on the absolute necessity of "the union of the figure with the background. The Right interpretation is that the Colours of the Principal Object are to dispose themselves throughout the Picture & while every part is separated, the Eye is to feel a Harmony & Union throughout — the Back ground is to grow out of the principal figure in fact." Chinnery here as elsewhere heavily underscores words or phrases of particular importance.

On another occasion he chides his pupil "You have rode faster than your Horse — with all your Talent you have to learn something of patience & method — this latter most particularly & altho' things are well done without method, nothing masterly ever (underscored three times) was done without it — Every thing without it must look bungled — the lesson is that it ever will be bungled in spite of ever so much Genius! Don't think this is Talk — it is the fact arising from the small Experience of 25 years.

" . . . In all cases — in every picture that is painted of any kind in miniature the process is

Chinnery's sketches in India include many of huts in the countryside and these two were drawn in Bengal.

— Courtesy Victoria and Albert Museum

28

Form (the model) Shadows (of all limbs) Tinting . . . this is the leading Feature of the process of every picture – & without wh, no picture can really succeed as a masterly work.

"There is an axiom very difficult to persuade even the professor of, much more the Amateur – but I will give it to you & if you profit by it I shall be glad – it is this – that nothing can be done well from nature that is not equally well done without it – Colouring most particularly – If you can feel this, it will teach you to do as I have done.

"Make continual & repeated Studies in Theory & adapt this to practice – The evil of the Art is Science – the Flowers only are Art – remember all this & when people talk of painting with their Eye, it is not the organ we see & see with on a clear day a mile on on the Horizon, but the mind's Eye, the Poets Eye, that is equal to embrace the cause as well as the Effect."   Born teacher though he was, even Chinnery was forced to admit that in the last analysis "it is air, grace and something not very describable which makes pictures."[5] And again: "Let ability be ever so great 9/10ths of our Art is Mechanical & depends on Means very far distant from the Original powers wh set it going."   Chinnery is conscious of the somewhat haranguing tone of his letters for he tells her: "I think I hear you say: 'if this man will be writing his long notes, why don't he send a ready made Half hour to read them in."

If Chinnery was on the whole tactful he also knew when to be blunt.   "Excellent!" he begins in one letter, but then adds "But you have got into a mess wh I don't know how to cure by writing – & till I see you nothing can be done effectively."   He advised her about the background to a painting in these terms: "It must always be cool & never approach the warmth of the head, however, for the sake of harmony a warm coloured head may radiate with the ground but generally the thing must be cool and kept back."   On colours he expressed his liking for vermilion – "There is something about vermilion – very curious – vermilion is vermilion".   It is an often-quoted statement of Chinnery's because he uses the colour so frequently to highlight special features.

Chinnery's often rambling and sometimes bombastic correspondence is revealing not only for his views on painting and for his talents as a teacher but for the light they throw on his moods and temperaments.   In 1817 he had evidently been teased by Mrs Browne about the forthcoming visit of a younger artist, William Havell, who arrived in Calcutta from China in 1817.[6]   Chinnery replies: "About Mr H. he is not yet here – I believe he has not yet come up from the ship – Fear me not – you have no Idea how tough a Battle I shall make if there is any need of it – Any flourish of trumpets preceding king this or king that in any Tragedy you ever saw is a Child's rattle to the ushering in this Hero of the Art – I have the funniest story to tell you you ever heard – I have been sounded as to my reception of him more than once & have given my opinion just as I ought to give it – If he is a clever man I shall be really glad to see him – delighted indeed, for having to contend with sound masculine ability is always to be courted – it is only your pretenders & half wits that are annoying.

"But I have a tolerably accurate notion of my own powers & to put me out of the saddle would be a job not easily accomplished rest assured – there are not 3 people I would say this much to, & do not give it as my opinion – I wd not seem arrogant for the whole world . . . There is such a thing as Galvanizing Talent as well as other things & if this Youngster comes in contact so as to have a chance of taking a single picture from me I shall get my Back pretty well up – from the novelty I must suffer something of course; but when this is over you shall find that if my Art (& God knows I have nothing else to build on!) has been the means of having such Friends as you & many others about me, I will shew myself worthy of attention & Distinction that are my greatest pride – But I have not studied (three times underlined) 25 Years for nothing not for a little – so never fear – there are not 6 at home even who I would stand in any awe of – but don't say I said so – I only say this much to give you confidence that I feel my ground safely."

We read of Chinnery's somewhat hectic social life when in declining Mrs Browne's invitation he writes: "My kind thanks about today – I dine with the noble Lord at 5 & am prevented accepting your obliging invitation & tho' I declare I will be quiet, go nowhere, drink Tea & be stupid in private, still the week is again filled up! It is all very flattering but my vanity & my Conscience are continually at Loggerheads.   When I consider . . . that every hour of my Life ought to be devoted to my Studies I think I do wrong even to stir."   On another occasion in 1816 Chinnery who had a reputation of being a non-drinker confessed that "one solitary Glass of Champagne half killed me & occasioned all the real pain I underwent."

Illness, real or imagined, seemed a constant tribulation. In 1814 Chinnery was "undergoing the most abominable operation possible, the largest Tooth in my Head being extracted (begging your pardon for talking on so prosaic a Circumstance) by that most capital Operator Mr Shuter who I must recommend to your notice when you are unwell again with Tooth Ache."   In a letter in 1817 he wrote of a recurring affliction which affected his eyesight in India and later Macau: "At 8 I must be before the Easel, unwell as I am & have been, with hardly the power of knowing one end of the pencil's stick from the other – but as I am doing more than any man ever did I imagine, & am certainly doing more than any man ought – shortly some relief must be afforded me, or my Career will be at an end pretty decidedly – An immense exertion must be made & I am making it."   In 1821 he was writing: "I have been laid up these 4 last days, & am still so, with 30 Boils on my left Leg the Torture of wh is excessive & mentally I am in misery from the necessary suspension of my Business!   However tomorrow well or unwell I must make the effort & go down stairs to my painting room."

Gradually, Mrs Chinnery, who arrived in Calcutta in 1818, creeps into the correspondence. Chinnery in 1820 thanks Mrs Browne for an invitation to them both; "Very many thanks about Wednesday from Mrs C & myself – but she trusts you will excuse her in the morning – in the Evening she will accompany me & be happy to see you."   In this and other references to his wife there is no hint of any animosity or coldness by Chinnery and it would seem that at this stage of their life they were on cordial terms.

These are mere fragments of an extensive correspondence. The treatise amplifies many of the points in the letters and a full transcription has now been published.[7]

5

Triumph and Tragedy

"THE greatest painter we have had in Calcutta since the days of Zoffany" was how the Friend of India described George Chinnery. And in the early years of the 19th century he was the latest in a long line of painters in oil and water colours who had come to India both as portraitists and to cash in on the new vogue in Britain for the "picturesque".[1] Tilly Kettle arrived in Madras in 1769 and stayed seven years, John Zoffany came in 1783 and spent six years and Arthur Devis who came in 1785 spent 10 years. John Smart and Ozias Humphry also preceded Chinnery and were highly regarded.

Among the patrons of these artists were the British administrators as well as Indian potentates and Robert Home was commissioned to paint a number of pictures for the rulers of Oudh during the years that Chinnery was painting in Calcutta. These artists painted in oil though water-colours enjoyed popularity from which were made engravings, aquatints and lithographs. William Hodges and Thomas and William Daniell were active in the last two decades of the 18th century and these artists contributed greatly to the cult of the picturesque in Britain and gave the people their first glimpse – albeit somewhat romantic and idealised – of life in India. In its wake, amateur sketching became popular, as we have seen in a previous chapter when D'Oyly lived in Dacca. These amateurs were answering a need which is now fulfilled by photography and it is interesting to speculate how many more of us today would be sketching but for the advent of the mass-produced camera.

For Chinnery, however, his arrival in India opened up immediate and fruitful avenues of work. Many of his predecessors had achieved fame and made good money – Zoffany particularly, for he is said to have made £10,000 from his various commissions, while the Daniells who went to India by way of Macau in 1786 made an equally impressive income.

Chinnery had one advantage, however, and that was his artistic versatility. He could use virtually any medium and could paint large portraits, miniatures, water colours and gouaches as well as sketch in pencil, ink and sepia. Moreover, it was a time of affluence when "civil servants and princely merchants distributed their rupees with less reluctance than their successors part with their pice." His arrival in Calcutta from Dacca in 1812 resulted in almost immediate commissions, and in June of that year he painted a miniature of Sir George Nugent, the Commander-in-chief and following that he received a commission to paint the Governor-General, Lord Minto. One of these survives today in the Town Hall of the Scottish border town of Hawick. A replica was sent to Batavia and later came into the possession of Sir Stamford Raffles, founder of Singapore, and yet another replica was hung in the residence of the Colonial Secretary in that colony. We are told[2] that another two portraits were painted, one seated, for the Dutch inhabitants of Batavia "at their request in 1814" and another was bought by Lord Curzon for Calcutta's Victoria Memorial Hall.

In 1814, Chinnery was back to miniature painting again, this time with a picture of Sir Robert Rollo Gillespie [3] who as a Major-General was to lose his life the same year through his "indiscreet daring" in assaulting the mountain-fortress of Kalanga in the Anglo-Nepal war. Another important work that year was a water-colour of Richmond Thackeray, his wife and his celebrated son, William Makepeace. This is a charming picture which shows young William sitting on top of a pile of five tomes which have been placed on a table, with his arms around his attractive dark-eyed young mother, fondling a ribbon on her dress. Seated at the right is a somewhat elongated Richmond Thackeray. The celebrated author was later to mention Chinnery in his novel *The Newcomes* when the Colonel refers to a drawing done by his son, an art student. He says: "Why, the rascal, Sir, has drawn me, his own father! And I have sent the drawing to Major Hobbs, who is in command of my regiment. Chinnery himself, Sir, couldn't hit off a likeness better."

In the same year, a pencil and water-colour portrait of an unknown officer was produced by Chinnery and survives today in the National Gallery of Scotland and this was one of a large number of commissions he undertook in the following year from people in many walks of life. Alas, no detailed record is known to survive of all the commissions he performed or the prices he charged, and only some of the more distinguished sitters can be identified.

In 1815, Calcutta celebrated the victory at Waterloo with all the fervour and loyalty that comes from having rubbed shoulders with the great man himself. For the Duke had come to India in 1798 with his brother, Richard Wellesley as Governor-General and the two had done much to bolster the prestige of the British empire, particularly Arthur, who at the age of 33 had been made a Major-General and achieved victories over the Marathas at Assaye and Argaon a year later. This was described by a historian [4] as "a triumph more splendid than any recorded in Deccan history." Among the decorations erected at the festive gathering in Calcutta was a transparency placed over the North Gate of Government House, representing the Duke of Wellington on horseback from a design by Chinnery.

The next distinguished sitter was the new Governor-General, the Marquess of Hastings and contemporary accounts [5] tell us that "Mr Chinnery has commenced upon the whole-length picture of the Rt. Hon. the Earl of Moira (Lord Hastings) for which His Lordship was solicited some time ago to sit by the Masonic Lodge at the Isle of France. His Lordship is represented in the magnificent robes of the Garter, surrounded by the emblems of masonry. The likeness is already correct and striking." This painting was apparently sent to Mauritius, and was one of a number of Vice Regal portraits he undertook.

Chinnery was also asked to paint at least one other portrait of Lord Hastings, an equestrian composition, but although a sum of 16,000 rupees had been raised for the picture, at a meeting held in the Calcutta Town Hall on July 9, 1827, it was stated that "at the end of two years, Mr Chinnery not having fulfilled his part of the engagement, the committee withdrew from it entirely".[6] There was another portrait of the same Governor-General painted at an unknown date showing him three-quarter length, which hung in the Viceroy's House at Delhi for many years.[7] It is also believed Chinnery painted a portrait of his wife, the Marchioness of Hastings, for the Calcutta Agricultural and Horticultural Society of which she was patroness. It is reported [8] that Chinnery wrote to the Society stating that the picture would be ready towards the end of 1823 and the next reference to it was its exhibition at the Calcutta Brush Club when the critic of the Literary Gazette found it "vulgar and unpleasing".

32

Lord Hastings was succeeded by the Senior Member of Council, Mr John Adam, and of course one of the first acts of a loyal British community was to invite him to sit for a portrait by Chinnery. A subscription list was opened and although almost 16,000 rupees was collected Chinnery did not get further than a few imperfect sketches [9] — and "the painter's habitual procrastination was blamed".

It would seem that Calcutta society was familiar with Chinnery's moods for they decided to send home his sketches to Sir Thomas Lawrence and commission him to paint the picture. Adam had since died on his way to England. Lawrence completed the picture and contemporary newspaper reports [10] record the arrival of the picture and its public exhibition in the Town Hall. One curious omission was noted, however. Adam habitually wore glasses and Chinnery's sketches showed him wearing them. At first Lawrence included them but was apparently dissatisfied with the result and painted them out. Adam was not there to complain. Chinnery had long ago left for Macau and Canton. A new Governor-General had taken up office and the portrait of Adam took its place in Government House, Calcutta and was later moved to Delhi. [11]

Among others whom Chinnery painted at this time was Sir Edward Paget, who was to write to his wife Harriet in May, 1825 "Chinnery is so uncertain a fellow that I have no dependence upon his promises. He likes landscape painting a thousand to one better than portrait painting, except when he gets so fine a subject (tell that to Caroline) as myself. Then he gets quite inspired". Two years earlier, before leaving for Serampore, Chinnery had painted Sir Edward's wife and five children, a charming family portrait which caused Paget days of anxiety when the artist failed to deliver the picture on time.

Between February 8, 1823, when Sir Edward wrote "I do not think I shall have the patience to let many days over my head without hunting him up" and February 19 when in desperation he wrote "Five o'clock and my picture not arrived! Oh, fie, my dear Mr Chinnery! . . .", he was constantly in a dither of anticipation.

It arrived the next day and he records that "upon my return from my drive yesterday I found Mr Chinnery in the act of hanging the picture of my beloved darlings. It is perfectly, perfectly lovely, and a comfort and pleasure to me not to be described. He has in truth, done his interesting subject justice". [12] Paget was one of two commanders-in-chief Chinnery painted, the other being Nugent, and it would appear that in addition to this portrait, and the family group the artist also painted a miniature, possibly of Lady Paget, for he wrote about asking Chinnery "to do something to the drapery of the miniature".

Another of Chinnery's subjects was an Indian nabob, Raja Protap Chand, the son of the Maharajadhiraj Bahadur Tej Chand of Burdwan, who died in the following January. Fourteen years later, however, a person turned up claiming to be the Raja and this led to a celebrated court case. The claimant was put on trial charged with impersonation and rioting and Chinnery's portrait was brought down from the Palace at Burdwan and kept in a room adjoining the Court where it was shown to the witnesses who came forward to testify to their acquaintance with the original. [13]

It is necessary, however, to return to the year 1816 — the year in which Chinnery had written to Mrs Browne, his pupil "I feel my ground safely". He decided at that time that he would resume his family life though he would implement the reunion in stages.

We have brief glimpses of the family in England at Gilwell Hall in the memoirs of Madame Vigée Lebrun, the French portraitist who visited the Chinnerys and heard "the two little angels" sing while Mrs Chinnery played the piano. Incidentally, the visitor found Mrs Chinnery

This oil painting by Chinnery shows a village scene in India.

"good-looking" – an opinion Chinnery himself was to contradict frequently in later years. [14]

It was the daughter, Matilda, who was to proceed first to Calcutta, however, and the Court of Directors of the East India Company, "in exercise of their right to control the entry of European women into India, ordered that Miss Matilda Chinnery be permitted to proceed to her father in Calcutta". [15]   She sailed out on the *Minerva* on July 31 1817.   Two years later she was married to James Cowley Brown of the Bengal Civil Service.   Chinnery painted their portraits and whatever the truth about Mrs Chinnery's appearance certainly his daughter had a soft, attractive face, large dark eyes and a slim, neat figure.

The reunion seems to have been a success for in March the following year, the Court granted permission for Mrs Marianne Chinnery to proceed to her husband in Calcutta.   She was allowed to take out a maidservant named Anne Cavanagh. [16]   Mrs Chinnery travelled on the ship, *Henry Porcher* in April.

Three years later, Chinnery's son, John, arrived in India.   If their arrival ushered in a period of domestic bliss, it was short-lived and in the next four years he was to experience a run of tragedy and bad luck that was to drive him from India almost on the verge of a nervous breakdown.   Reference has already been made in the previous chapter to Chinnery's bouts of indifferent health and on top of this he had a reputation for instability; indeed at times of stress he showed signs of being a manic-depressive. [17]

These bouts produced a man of unpredictable moods and we see him at times terribly cocksure of himself and vain, and at other times cast down and dispirited.   One writer [18] says that his mercurial temperament made him veer between extreme optimism and abject self-pity.   Chinnery had, however, been devoted to his family, particularly his children, and had sent them remittances of money as well as paintings.   But he soon found that the years that had divided them had created an unbridgeable gulf and when in 1819 his daughter Matilda married, Chinnery found himself having to contend with a wife who was clearly dismayed at the change she found in him.

She soon discovered the existence of his mistress (whether the liaison was still active at that time is uncertain) as well as the two illegitimate children though she clearly forgave him by deciding to have the children, now aged about seven, baptised by the Senior Chaplain at the Presidency of Fort William. [19]   But if this were not enough she found her husband's life style so changed that it was impossible to pick up the broken threads of their marriage.   The succession of sumptuous feasts they were asked to attend where the tables "groaned beneath the weight of everything in season" and her husband's extravagant and eccentric ways must have made life very difficult.

In fairness to Chinnery he had been involved in a large expense in bringing his wife to India.   Not only had he paid her passage and put up a surety for her but he provided the money to bring out a European maid with her and he also had to pay the maid's return fare to England – all this was necessary to ensure that neither would be a burden to the East India Company. [20]   Added to this he had to maintain his wife, daughter and son and pay for their education, as well as his Indian mistress and the two sons he had by her.

It was probably in part his financial worries which so quickly brought to an end his married life in India. [21]   His well-known eccentricities must have made him a trying husband and as one commentator adds: "Few therefore will incline wholly to blame Mrs Chinnery for the failure of the marriage.   Before she had been long in India he had again developed a violent antipathy for her." [22]

What must have been the final crushing blow was the tragedy which overtook his son.

John Eustace Chinnery had applied to go to India in 1821 and his father had obtained a promise from Lord Hastings, whose portrait he had painted, of a junior commission in the army. John applied to the East India Company in October of that year to proceed to Bengal to take up the appointment. The Directors, however, wanted proof that the nomination had been confirmed at home and a week later he was told at Horse Guards in London that the Commander-in-chief had given the commission to someone else.[23]

We can understand his bitter disappointment but he pressed his application to live with his parents. This, however, the Court of the East India Company refused to sanction. Despite the rebuff, he managed to get to India where within a short time he contracted a tropical fever and died. That was on June 10, 1822. Chinnery was heart-broken.

The grave is at Berhampore and the following inscription is to be found on a tablet fixed to the north wall of the cemetery: "Erected to the memory of a most beloved and affectionate son by his disconsolate, affectionate and most afflicted father as a tribute to that worth, those principles and amiable dispositions which had it pleased the Almighty to have spared him to the world would have been the honour of his own life and the happiness of a family left inconsolable by his premature death."[24]

There is no reason to doubt the statement in one book that "the death of his son overwhelmed the artist." Chinnery's inscription mentions only "a most afflicted father". The mother's grief is ignored as if her feelings were of no account. An invitation shortly after by Dr Joshua Marshman at the Baptist Missionary College at Serampore gave Chinnery the chance to escape from his grief, his wife and his increasingly demanding debt collectors. Serampore, then a Danish trading station, east of Calcutta and beyond British jurisdiction, was only an interlude. He had found only a temporary haven and not the peace of mind he yearned for and while there Chinnery made plans to leave India, his wife and his debts and get far away from them all. No doubt, Marshman was able to tell his guest a good deal about Macau for many of his Chinese students came from that city.

His debts at that time were said to be running at about £40,000 and his state of mind can be guessed.[25] Whether Chinnery hoped to clear himself of part of this burden by taking on a number of Vice-Regal commissions is not clear, though from contemporary reports the Establishment of Calcutta still considered him pre-eminent as a painter and continued to offer him work. However, an old acquaintance[26] believed these "differences with his creditors" was one of the main reasons for leaving. Chinnery evidently realised that with the indifferent health he had been experiencing in the last few years he would have to leave India altogether. Besides, he was also fed up with the bowing and scraping that seemed part and parcel of life there. He often spoke derisively about the snobbery in this rank and status-conscious society. He was later to tell a friend in Macau[27] that the aristocracy was to be compared with "laudanum and salts, which when taken moderately have good effect, but take too much of either and you know the consequences, extremely dangerous and disagreeable."

He also spoke of Europeans who "suffered severe curvature of the spine" from excessive bowing. Shortly after his death in Macau, W. C. Hunter came across a choice oil painting among Chinnery's possessions. It showed the Bund at Calcutta with a ship's boat lying alongside and a Lascar crew preparing to pull out to a ship moored in the river. In the distance was Calcutta and in the foreground was a European with a serious curvature of the spine, a portfolio under one arm and a sola topee in hand bowing to the city. At the top of the painting was a scroll in which were the words "Thermometer 200°, too hot for me." That was Chinnery's final epitaph to India.

Marianne Chinnery

— Courtesy National Gallery of Ireland

Colonel James Achilles Kirkpatrick

— Courtesy Hongkong and Shanghai Banking Corpn

The Kirkpatrick children

Calcutta waterfront

— Courtesy Hongkong and Shanghai Banking Corpn

Family group, Macau

— Courtesy Hongkong and Shanghai Banking Corpn

6

Between India and China

ONE of the more frequent criticisms of Chinnery's work, particularly in his last years in India, was his unreliability and his reluctance to finish his paintings. A former resident of Calcutta has been quoted[1] as saying that he could rarely be induced to complete his pictures. "After having satisfied himself with a masterly representation of the countenance he would turn to a new subject. Had he employed an assistant to complete the figure and fill in the drapery he would have made a much larger income." Nor was this an isolated criticism. The Bengal Hurkaru said "we have heard that he was as little to be depended upon for a promised painting as Coleridge was for a promised poem or lecture. He worked only by fits and starts."

On his death, an obituary in the newspaper, the Friend of India, said that in Calcutta he had been making almost 50,000 rupees a year and might have earned much more "if he could have brought himself to finish his pictures". Once, it added, he had completed the face he would put off the drudgery of painting in the accessories with the result that at the time of his departure he had on hand from 50 to 100 unfinished canvases. It is possible that in an effort to clear his heavy burden of debt Chinnery took on many more commissions than he could possibly complete; ill-health and depression caused by domestic worries could have been aggravating factors, though curiously three paintings considered his best were all undertaken in his last three years in India. These were Sir Francis Macnaghten, Puisne Judge of the Calcutta High Court, completed in 1824, Robert Cutlar Fergusson, Advocate General of Calcutta and Dr Joshua Marshman, the missionary at Serampore. As the Friend of India said "those who had had an opportunity of comparing the three pictures with the originals, will fully understand how his labours must have been appreciated." Moreover a respected critic of Chinnery's paintings says that after 15 years' study "I have yet to see a Chinnery oil unfinished or varying in style. When people talk about these qualities, it invariably means the oil is said to be Chinnery but is not . . . most of the attributing is done by dealers who have neither technical nor historical knowledge."[2]

Before following Chinnery to Macau, however, it is necessary to pause and take stock of his position at this stage of his career. As will be recalled from a previous chapter, Chinnery not unfairly placed himself among the top six in Britain. (In shorthand notes elsewhere he refers to four – Lawrence, Hoppner, Romney and Mrs Mee. Turner would surely rank as a fifth). Sir Charles D'Oyly accorded him top place among western artists in India and this was not the prejudiced opinion of a close friend but a balanced assessment of his skill by a brother artist.

Another modern critic[3] describes him as "the leading portraitist of the day" in India, while

Another official portrait which was widely acclaimed in Calcutta was Chinney's portrait of the Puisne Judge, Sir Francis Macnaghten.

another [4] said: "If he did not achieve the greatest heights, he nevertheless holds a high place in the second rank as a portrait and landscape painter. The diversity and vitality of his draughtsmanship and the range and charm of his colour will always ensure for him a particular niche in the history of British art."

According to the Friend of India "he was the greatest painter we have had in Calcutta since the days of Zoffany". The Times art critic, reviewing a Chinnery exhibition in London in 1932 felt "he was not a great artist – not even in the same rank as Zoffany, Ozias Humphry and Arthur Devis, who also worked in India – but he was lively and entertaining and he had a good eye for a picture." The Bengal Hurkaru was not enthusiastic about his "hard and stiff style" but acknowledged his genius and said that had he been a steady and prudent man Chinnery might have accumulated in Calcutta an enormous fortune and lived luxuriously while that fortune was being made.

Chinnery scores, however, not just on the undisputed quality of his major works, but, as has been mentioned, on his versatility in various media. He was particularly noteworthy for his prolific sketching in pencil and ink, and it is likely that he learnt the relationship between sketching, composition and painting from his contemporaries and tutors. He apparently sketched in this way in an effort to achieve perfection – hence also his shorthand notes to elaborate on points in his pictures.

It might well have been better for him to have accepted fewer assignments and supplemented his main work with teaching – for which he had an undoubted talent – and in this way he might have gained a higher professional reputation and been more successful financially and this in turn might have resulted in a more stable and settled life. He was not made this way, however, and could not escape his own undisciplined whims and impulses, much less the attractive commissions which flooded into his studios. Too often heart ruled head and while this produced some great art, yet by overtaxing himself he did, according to contemporary accounts, occasionally drain himself of inspiration.

Apart from his portraits Chinnery has left us some exciting canvases of seascapes and landscapes of India, particularly the shoreline of Calcutta, reminiscent as they are of Turner, as well as scenes from the Hooghly and Ganges Rivers. His pictures of the Thackeray family and Colin Robertson Larkins and his servant, are works of great sensitivity and delicacy, while his sketches achieved a realism and faithfulness that few other artists in India could emulate.

Chinnery made known his preference for landscape painting in 1825 even though there was little money in it. Once again we turn to the Bengal Hurkaru for a comment: "His Indian landscapes are truly excellent and were greatly and highly valued by his brother artists at home . . . we have heard them spoken of with generous and earnest admiration." His sketches were considered by one admirer in Calcutta as works of "rare genius."

Yet it is as a portraitist that he is chiefly judged. Of those that are undoubtedly his it can be said that he perfected a style that stamps him as an artist who caught the character and personality of the sitter much more vividly than the mere likeness. This is indeed what distinguished Chinnery from his contemporaries in China where there had been a flourishing Chinese school long before his departure for Macau.

In China, western sailing ships had been calling at Macau since the middle of the 16th century and Jesuit priests had been painting in Macau and China from the 17th century. Castiglione and his colleagues had made a name for themselves in Chien Lung's court in Peking and had introduced a number of European techniques which were adopted by the Court painters. Between 1715 and 1766 Castiglione painted courtiers of three reigns, including the emperor's favourite concubine in the costume of Madame de Pompadour. But the impression these paintings made was fairly limited and the Chinese artists for the most part remained faithful to their classical styles. It was not until much later that they saw any virtue in western art forms and the chief influence was not artistic superiority so much as cold cash.

A large number of European artists were in Canton and Macau before 1815.[5] Some of the most prominent were Thomas Daniell who with his nephew William were in China before going to India in 1786, William Alexander and Thomas Hickey on Lord Macartney's mission to China, and young John Webber, who at 24 was chosen to accompany Captain Cook on his third voyage of exploration, succeeding William Hodges on earlier expeditions. Webber, the son of a Swiss sculptor living in London, visited Macau in 1779. Another artist on this same expedition was William Ellis, who signed on as surgeon's second mate, but was also a skilled landscape painter and a natural history draughtsman.[6]

When William Alexander visited Canton with Lord Macartney's expedition on December 7, 1793, this young British artist encountered two Chinese painters, Puqua and Camfon, and he wrote that they "copy accurately and produce very highly finished pictures, indifferently coloured, from the prints of Bunbury, Kauffman & c and many prints of this style were seen there for that purpose. They have no knowledge of the theory of art or any pretensions beyond imitation, their productions (generally speaking) are labour merely, without genius, they work when possible by mechanical processes, the lines of buildings & c are made with a ruler, and the subjects they execute are multiplied by tracery & c, they have no notion of perspective or the appearance of lines, nor of the reflection of objects in water. When they undertake a portrait they seldom please, nor have the taste to flatter, the subject is copied individually."

He also met a Chinese sculptor who claimed to "savy missa Banks welly well" – this was Thomas Banks, the English classical sculptor. Alexander continued: "This man modelled small busts of officers which would have been very well had not the bad taste of his employers required them to be coloured with blue coats, red cheeks and powdered hair which quite spoilt them. On his door front was written 'Handsome Face Maker' as a good recommendation."[7]

Alexander does not mention another Chinese painter active in Canton at the time. He laboured under the unflattering name of Spoilum; history does not record whether this was a hilarious English attempt to pronounce his Chinese name or one given him by an irate customer. He worked in Canton from 1785 to 1810 and in 1789 he painted the Hawaiian royal visitor, Tianna, and it was stated that "the painter had indeed most faithfully represented the lineaments of his countenance."[8]

Spoilum painted a number of western traders, sea captains and Chinese merchants and one of his best known works was of the Chinese silk merchant, Eshing, now in the Peabody Museum in Salem, Massachusetts. It is distinctive in several respects and reflects the work of a Chinese artist moving into the Western style of painting from traditional flat portraiture.[9]

From Alexander's comments and from observations of Spoilum's paintings it is clear that the early Chinese artists of the western school picked up their techniques from copying and there is also evidence of copies being made of American and Chinese frames.

Spoilum however was superior to his contemporaries. He painted eyes of great sensitivity and he had, what one writer described as, "an excellent feeling for the personality of the sitter."[10] The background of the portrait was invariably relatively flat and this flatness was reminiscent of the native style of portraiture. Spoilum held sway for a number of years and did a thriving business and had a definite influence on other Chinese painters of the time.

The Chinese were also prolific painters of landscapes, though these were notable for their lack of understanding of perspective and their invariable flatness and this persisted for many years until Chinnery arrived. Human figures were often characterised by their stiffness and rigidity and their lack of naturalness. Moreover these artists thought nothing of painting a river or harbour scene showing ships being propelled by the wind in one direction with flags or pennants blowing in the other. And while these make charming (and today very expensive) souvenirs of this historic period in Sino-western relations, they demonstrate that landscape painting in the western style was in its infancy when Chinnery arrived.

The Chinese medium of painting was either in ink on silk or paint on paper, wood, ivory or other material and it is clear that mastery of the new medium of canvas did not come easily. Nor was the paint durable and many surviving oils show evidence of excessive cracking and flaking. Pencil sketches were rare and the western approach to draughtsmanship was a science that was unfamiliar to the Chinese artist.

How Chinnery helped speed a change that was beginning to take place we shall see in a later chapter. In 1825, Chinnery boarded the *Hythe,* a vessel built five years earlier and displacing 1425 tons. She was commanded by Captain J. Wilson and owned by Charles Marjoribanks who was to be President of the Select Committee of the East India Company in Canton four years later. She sailed from Calcutta on February 15, 1825 and touched at Penang on the way to Macau. When Chinnery left he was accompanied by his Indian servant, according to the ship's log, and the impression among some in Calcutta was that his sea-trip was dictated by health reasons. [11]

The Calcutta Monthly Journal 18 months later, reported that "the friends of Mr Chinnery will be glad to hear that his health has been re-established by his voyage to China, and that he has added greatly to his sketch book since he left Calcutta where, ere long, we hope circumstances will admit of his returning." Whether this report was inspired by some despairing creditor or by some remark or letter by Chinnery himself is not known. The artist, however, showed no inclination to return, except for a brief and torrid interlude during the Opium wars when he wrote to James Matheson: "If there was a ship going to Bengal, I would lock up my House today & be away could I most certainly!" Even then, Chinnery remained in China and the following chapters will concentrate on the 27 years of his life spent there.

This self-portrait by George Chinnery is one of a number he painted during his life-time.

7

The choice of Macau

W HEN Chinnery made his decision to live in Macau it was not the only haven in the Far East but it was perhaps the most civilised; it numbered English-speaking people among its population who were wealthy and sophisticated and, most important, it was beyond the reach of the courts in Calcutta.

Penang, an island off the west coast of Malaya near the head of the Straits of Malacca, had a more pleasant climate than Calcutta. But it was not as healthy as it looked and "for a Calcutta European it was considered the back of beyond with few of the amusements available in the other Presidency towns."[1] The more serious objection to Penang was that being subordinate to the Governor-General in India, a fugitive might be vulnerable to legal action for debts and also would have been within easy reach of an importunate wife.

Moreover while palm-fringed beaches might be a strong point in its favour to a present-day tourist, Chinnery was not looking for that kind of a change. He has been likened by some writers to Gauguin, who found his peace in the exile of Tahiti after a hectic life in Paris, but while "the magnetic pull of the exotic"[2] might have influenced both artists to forsake their native lands, Chinnery enjoyed his creature comforts, good company and the expatriate existence of an English gentleman. While he pursued the picturesque in painting with a zeal and devotion that inspires admiration, apart from his early years in Ireland he was not dedicated to exploring new styles and he remained fundamentally a traditionalist.

Another possibility for Chinnery might have been Malacca, further to the south. This port had been once Portuguese, then Dutch, then British in 1795, reverted to being Dutch in 1816 and was transferred back to Britain in 1824. Further south still, Singapore had been founded in 1819 but as neighbouring Johore had been under Dutch rule, its status was not confirmed until March 17, 1824 and it was still relatively raw and undeveloped. As in Penang, moreover, an absconding debtor might well feel the long arm of the Calcutta authorities uncomfortably close in either of these ports.

Macau suffered from none of these disadvantages. Although the East India Company directors lived there and maintained godowns, the city remained firmly under Portuguese rule. It had the further advantage of being near the city of Canton which offered even greater security in that it remained officially closed to foreign women and viewed with undisguised contempt any but its own rules and laws.

From connections in Calcutta, and particularly at Dr Marshman's college in Serampore, Chinnery had heard of the comfortable existence in Macau, the active social life and the wealth of the merchants and realised the bountiful opportunities for handsome commissions. While its summer was long, hot and humid, it enjoyed the respite of a short, cool winter and being on a

Chinnery's portrait of Harriet Low, who compiled a diary of her life in Macau from 1829 to 1833 when she lived there with her uncle, an American businessman from Boston, Massachusetts, and her aunt.

promontory it was well served with sea breezes. Among some in Calcutta, it had the reputation of a health resort. It also had shipping connections with the world in case further escape was necessary. In short it had almost everything Chinnery could want.

Chinnery arrived there on September 29, 1825, and he would have been lucky to have missed rough weather beating up the South China Sea at that time of year. We are left to wonder whether it was sea-sickness that kept the painter idle during the many weeks he spent at sea – or was it the memories of his last unhappy years in Calcutta, tinged perhaps with remorse for what he had decided to put behind him. Suffice it to say, there are no known paintings or sketches from this period.

As the sailing ship *Hythe* moved into the quieter waters of the Pearl River, Chinnery had his first glimpse of his new haven, the curious Eurasian hybrid of Macau, then 270 years old, and like a southern Mediterranean town transplanted into an oriental setting. It was another world entirely from Calcutta and as if to symbolise the difference and the great divide between his old life and the new, a sharply defined line separated blue sea from brown estuary water at the approaches to Macau.

Apart from his many lively sketches, Chinnery has left no detailed written record of life in the city and while his paintings and drawings, if they could be assembled together, would present a fascinating composite portrait we have to turn to the written record of Miss Harriet Low for a more intimate glimpse of life there.

Harriet, who was described as a lively young girl just past her 20th birthday, travelled to Macau in the company of her uncle and aunt, Mr and Mrs Wm H. Low, on the *Sumatra,* leaving Salem, Massachusetts, on May 24, 1829 and arriving on September 9, almost four years after Chinnery first stepped ashore. She has left in her diary[3] a colourful and highly personalised description of life. She tells how her ship anchored first off the Leema Islands and then, the following day, put into Macau roads.

"There was a heavy sea and we were obliged to lower everything over the stern and you would have been amused to see us all tied into a chair and swung over the stern of the ship," she wrote.

She then described the waters around Macau: "There is an immense quantity of boats all about, in which whole families live, indeed two or three generations. The women steer the boat and frequently have an infant on their backs – and the poor little thing only has a shaking if it cries.

"One idea of the Chinese amuses me exceedingly; that is that a vessel cannot go without eyes. They therefore have a large eye painted on each side of the bow, which looks very singular, and if you ask them why, they say: 'Hi, yah, how can you see without eye?'

"Macau from the sea looks beautiful, with some most romantic spots. We arrived there about 10 o'clock, took sedan chairs and went to our house . . . the streets are narrow and irregular."

It was not long before she was casting scorn on the manners of Macau. "You have no idea how difficult it is to keep alive one's religious feelings here, or to pass Sunday in a proper manner; I read aloud one of Buckminster's[4] excellent sermons but had no sooner finished it and was feeling somewhat disposed to be serious, than four or five people called.

"They make calls here on their return from church. You see, there is no country like ours for religious principles. The Chinese pay no sort of regard to the sabbath, but go on with their work as usual."

On October 18, Harriet recorded that she "went for a walk yesterday with our coolie and he took us all round the Praya Grande, over a great hill and back through the town – a monstrous walk and for the first one it was terrible. The streets are intolerable – hilly, irregular and horribly paved. We met no one but Portuguese and Chinamen who annoyed us very much by their intent gaze. On our way, however, we saw two of their women with small feet. I was perfectly astonished. These women's feet were about the size of our little Charley's (a boy of three – Ed). Only think of a full-grown and rather fat person having such feet. I thought she must be in torture. But she walked apparently with the greatest of ease. Both women carried canes."

Another entry tells us that "the men here dress their hair most singularly, having the front of the head shaved close to the skin, while the hair is allowed to grow long on the back of the head and is braided from the top, and you almost always see them with a queue of hair hanging to the bottom of their trousers. They take great pride in the length of their hair."

Harriet tells of a visit to a friend's house – apparently the Fearons with whom Chinnery at one time stayed. "It is the most romantic place, is very extensive and abounds in serpentine walks. There is a beautiful view of the sea, and immense rocks and trees. In another part there is a cave in the rocks where the celebrated Camoens wrote his Lusiad. A bust of him stands in the cave. It is a wild and delightful spot."

She tells of meeting a young, good-looking doctor – Dr Colledge – "he is the best man I have seen yet. Everybody loves him and speaks well of him. He has been truly kind to us, and we are under great obligations to him. It is a shame that he is a bachelor!"

A few days later Harriet again visited the Fearons where she enjoyed herself very much. "You would be astonished to see your once diffident sis dancing the first quadrille, not without much urging. However you must know that I am the only spinster in the place and I am pulled about in every direction."

Harriet's daughter, Katharine Hillard, who edited the diary, tells us that "I have often heard my mother say that ladies were so scarce in Macau at the time that they were obliged to take a different partner for each figure of the quadrille."

The next day Harriet went to see the "theatricals" which included several scenes from Shakespeare's *The Merchant of Venice*. "We had a very good farce called *'Killing no murder'* and several other scenes from different plays." Between the scenes the gentlemen and ladies walked on the verandah – "I like their manner of fixing the supper tables here. They have small tables holding about 10 which makes it much more social."

Harriet amused herself in many ways – visiting, sight-seeing, reading and sketching which she found a "delightful employment." A few days later she was visiting an old resident, Mr Beale "where we were cordially received by the old gentleman and entertained beyond measure. He has an aviary filled with a most choice collection of birds. The bird of paradise is by far the most beautiful.[5] After we had looked at them enough we walked in the garden which is literally filled with plants and trees of the rarest kinds and has a pond filled with a great variety of gold-fishes. After six we took tea in Chinese style. Each one's tea is put into a covered cup till sufficiently steeped, and is then drunk without milk or sugar. That did not suit my taste for sweets."

Soon after her arrival, Harriet was visited by two members of the British community and Mowqua, the Hong merchant. "Mowqua is a great character. He had on his winter dress which is rather singular. The cap is blue in front, the crown scarlet, with a blue glass button on the top. The whole dress was blue of different shades. I asked why they did not let ladies go to Canton. He said: 'Too muchy man want to look.' He said too: 'Canton too

56

small; no walky.' He was very gallant, I assure you."

She then describes the race course which she visited four days later.

"The race ground is at what is called the Barrier, which prevents all foreigners from passing over that spot. The course is about three-quarters of a mile. It is a delightful place, and I was much amused by the novel scene. There was a temporary house of bamboo built for the ladies and . . . it was very interesting to look upon the motley group below us.

"Chinese of all descriptions dressed in their most singular costume, some with large basket hats, many of them with nothing on their heads but carrying a fan which they hold up to screen them from the sun. Some had bags on their backs in which they put their babies. The poor little things were knocked about in the crowd as if they had been so many bits of wood.

"Portuguese and Lascars were mixed with the Chinese and to hear the mixture of languages made me think of the confusion of Babel.

"Some of the races were very good and some large bets were made. We returned about seven and had a long discussion upon the merits of the English. We concluded that they had been extremely polite to us, but that it is necessary to treat them with some reserve, and that the men are a good-for-nothing set of rascals. Do not tell anybody, but all they care about is eating, drinking and frolicking." And Harriet here adds a marginal note "Quite a modest conclusion."

A few days later, she noted that "the ladies here dress a great deal and we do not pretend to vie with the English ladies in anything but good conduct."

A fortnight or so later, Harriet was the guest of one of the prominent English merchants, Mr Dent, at a play. "It was one of the drollest things you ever saw. Several of the scenes were painted by Mr Chinnery. The play was performed very well. Some parts were admirably done, but the most amusing were the female characters. Mr Chinnery was one, and they could not have chosen anybody less fit to perform a female part; but however ridiculous his appearance made much sport."

Early in December, Harriet received a letter from Canton telling of a great fire there which consumed 200 houses. "The Chinese will not put out a fire," she wrote. "They say it is Joss pigeon (God's business) and 'no can.' They are a most remarkable people."

On December 8 she went to see Chinnery. "He has some fine likenesses there. He is remarkably successful. How I wish that I had a little of the needful to put into the man's hand that he might take my beautiful phiz, that I might transport it across the great waters into your hands."

On December 25, Harriet was invited to a Christmas dinner given by the East India Company directors. She tells us "After conversing for a while I was led to an elegant table — everything on the table was splendid — a whole service of massive plate. There were about 60 at table. The dinner consisted of every delicacy served in the most elegant style and with the greatest order.

"Everyone brings their own servant to wait upon them at table. When the first course is cleared away, these extra servants all fall back to the wall and the regular servants carry out the dishes handed to them by the butlers. I think you would have been much entertained to look at this immense table, with the long row on each side, and to see the different expressions on the countenances of those whose business it was to eat and those whose business it was to look on.

"It would be impossible to describe the various dishes. Suffice it to say that everything was as elegant as possible . . . The time passed very pleasantly and there was nothing stiff about it. Everybody appeared perfectly easy and at home. After dinner the lights were extinguished

Chinnery used to make up sketchbooks complete with covers and a contents page in copper-plate handwriting and these two pictures show two covers. The first was drawn in 1826 for a sketchbook of Canton and the second apparently included views of both Macau and Canton and was drawn in 1836.

— Courtesy Victoria and Albert Museum

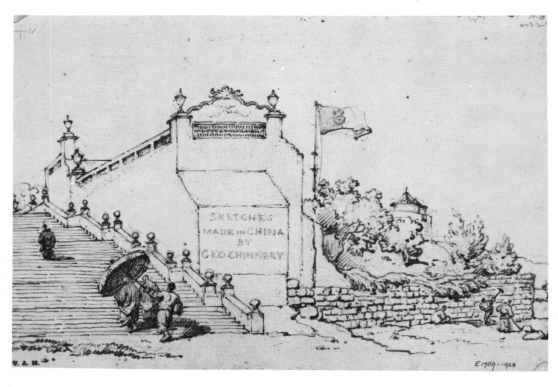

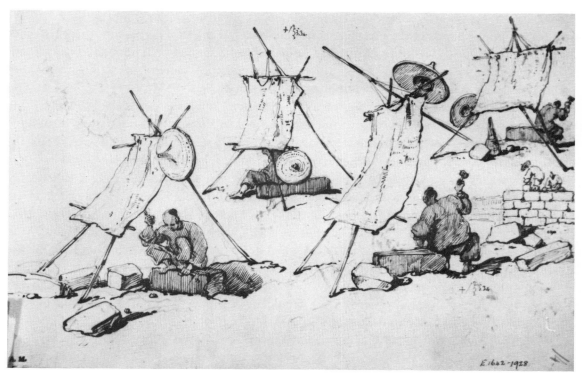

Chinnery invariably sketched his models from many angles. Above he illustrates the stone-mason at work behind his improvised sun shield and below, he shows a hawker carrying faggots of wood while a fisherman stands on a rock looking out to sea.

and the long table was covered with blue lights (dishes of burning brandy and salt – Ed). We were all to put our hands into these blue flames and pull out the raisins beneath. This is called snap dragon and is a favourite Christmas amusement in England. I thought I was in the infernal regions and I never shall forget the frightful visages of some of the gentlemen as they held the plates up near their faces. The effect is astonishing."

About a month later it was time for another festival, this time the Lunar New Year and Harriet records that "the compradore chin chind us not to ring the bell tomorrow, being their New Year's day. The Chinese have an idea it will call up Fanqui or the devil. They fire crackers all day for the purpose of keeping off the evil spirit for the coming year."

On February 3, Harriet dined with the security merchants – "they gave me a full account of their customs. Old Tinqua had the audacity to ask me how old I was. He says he has five wives. No 1 his father and mother chose for him. 'He no like No 1. Too much ugly.' No 2 'he likey. He choose her.' He is 62, but you would never think him more than 35. I thought I was paying him a great compliment when I told him so; but I hear that I could have said nothing more displeasing as they like to be considered old."

A month later Harriet was arranging to attend a tea party but "old Chinnery who is a monstrous epicure wished to know if there would be a supper or what they would have to eat. The reply was 'Toast and tea, and butter if it is to be had'."

Harriet did not say whether Chinnery joined them.

She wrote later of the British ladies who had slipped into Canton without permission, including Mrs Fearon and Mrs Baynes who told Harriet that when they first arrived the people had had boats stationed on the water and had paid three cash to see the "Fanqui women" – though there had been no disturbance.

She comments: "I think the Chinese are much more civil than either American or English people would have been if a Chinese woman with little feet had appeared in our streets dressed in the costume of her country. Why she would have been mobbed and hooted at immediately."

By April 29, she was visiting Chinnery's studio regularly and was copying some of his sketches.

The next month it was beginning to get warm and at an East India Company dinner she was delighted to find that "the luxurious punkah was going and kept us just cool enough."

On May 18, Harriet's 21st birthday, she was writing of making her own visit to Canton for although "the Chinese will never consent to ladies going, they will wink at it. As Mowqua told Uncle 'they will shutty eye and shutty ear'."

In November of 1830 she did visit Canton and was duly discovered by the Chinese inhabitants while she was walking in Old China Street. But no harm came to her. "Lights were called that the Chinamen might look at us. They kindled up fires in an instant to behold our faces and we had quite a rabble round us before we reached the front of the Factories again, though they were all perfectly civil and made no noise but only showed a little curiosity."

If Harriet's visit provoked curiosity among the Chinese inhabitants, the young woman from Salem found why the bachelors enjoyed their sojourn in Canton.

"You have no idea how elegantly these bachelors live. I don't wonder they like it," she wrote. But Harriet herself admitted in a later entry in her diary that while discussing transmigration after death, a Hong merchant told her that "if he should live again as a man he would be a Chinaman, but if a woman he would be an Englishwoman." The privileges were therefore not all one-sided.

A few months later she wrote that "the Empress of China is dead (or rather the mother of the Emperor) and all the people will have to mourn for 100 days; the men are not allowed to shave for that space of time, so we shall have beautiful looking sevants."

With summer came the rains and Harriet wrote that "it was raining in torrents, nothing to be seen but water, and the (sedan) chairs appeared to be swimming. The coolies with their enormous hats, wading up to their knees and with lanterns in their hands, presented a curious picture." [6]

Harriet "sallied forth with two gentlemen to meet my fate, with all the courage of a heroine, in the midst of thunder, lightning, rain and darkness and the roaring of the Chinamen, which exceeded the thunder, for they all holloa together and thereby hear nothing."

Yet later she spoke of a "strike" by Macau's ubiquitous sedan chair carriers. The local mandarins were applying pressure on them to raise more in dues — "it seems the mandarins have come short in meeting their expenses and so they have put an extra 'squeeze' upon the poor bearers and, until that is paid they forbid their carrying the chairs and their poor backs would suffer sadly did they disobey the order. We cannot help pitying the poor wretches who are subject to such tyranny."

This was the Macau of Chinnery's time — a vivid, eventful, mostly carefree life for the expatriates saved from being very superficial by the long hours spent each day following their own interests and hobbies — Harriet with reading and writing her diary, Chinnery with sketching and painting.

This is the setting for the following chapters which deal with the last 27 years of his life in Macau.

Chinnery's sketch of the letter-writer includes enlargements of the hand showing how the brush was held. It contains the following shorthand notes: "Drawn April 14th 1840. The head ought to be more to the man's right hand. Study of this required one writing one holding (the brush?) and taken from these . . . Both drawn and filled up at home May 8th '40."

The lower picture again shows enlargements of hands gripping various objects. Other drawings show a man pouring water from a bucket, while in the background is a fisherman pulling in a line over the praya wall.

8

Of missionaries and merchants

EVERY foreign vessel arriving in China in the early years of the 19th century dropped anchor first in the roads of Macau where they were boarded by a pilot. He made a note of the cargo, and the ship's boat then sailed to the Custom-house where a toll was paid. At the same time permission was sought to land any female passengers as Chinese regulations did not allow them to go to Whampoa. A "chop" or permit was then obtained to enable the vessel to move up the Pearl River, past the Bogue Forts and on to Whampoa.[1]

We know that Chinnery's vessel, the *Hythe,* made the customary stop at Macau but what is less certain is whether Chinnery left the ship there or proceeded direct to Canton and remained there for the winter, or alternatively put his baggage ashore and established a base in Macau before travelling up to Canton. It was clear to Chinnery that he would have to get down to work quickly. He apparently brought little money with him and left large debts and a wife whom he still had to support in Calcutta — if only to ensure that she did not follow him to Macau. These debts were to plague him for at least the next 16 years, as a letter in the archives of Jardine, Matheson and Co Ltd indicate.[2]

Not long after arriving he picked up a copy of the Bengal Hurkaru in Canton which contained a notice declaring him to be an absconding debtor. Characteristically, Chinnery made light of it and put on a display of mock indignation. He is quoted[3] as saying: "Was there ever such an insult. It is insufferable! 'Whereas George Chinnery, an absconding debtor, is hereby required . . . ' Debts! what are debts? Fiddlesticks to your debts. Think of George Chinnery, neither Mister nor Esquire; of George Chinnery, without head or tail; that is too much to bear!" While Chinnery's idiosyncracies aroused amusement among his fellow expatriates in Macau and Canton, he was regular in sending sums of money to Marianne, his wife, in Calcutta. Two years after his arrival Chinnery told a friend[4] as he posted a letter: "there goes another thousand rupees" and he added that he sent an annual sum as well "to keep her quiet".

To earn this money and to keep body and soul together, Chinnery was quick to make it known that he sought commissions. One of Chinnery's early sitters was the beautiful Elizabeth Noad Fearon, wife of Christopher Fearon, who was in partnership with James Ilberry in a firm known as Ilberry, Fearon & Co.[5] It has been said by some historians that Chinnery at first lived with the Fearons in Macau; however the family records put Christopher Fearon's arrival at 1826, in the year following Chinnery's. It has not yet been clarified where in Macau Chinnery lived immediately after his arrival though he did in later years move to a studio in Rua Ignacio Baptista. That he did stay with the Fearons at some time in his early years is generally accepted and he established a long-lasting friendship with them, not only painting a portrait of Mrs Fearon — it has been described[6] as "a beautiful oil" with the sitter wearing a dress with long feathery sleeves — but acting as Godfather to the Fearon's youngest child, Robert Inglis in 1837.

There are other portraits of Mrs Fearon, such as that owned by the Hongkong and Shanghai Banking Corporation, but there is some doubt about the attribution of this painting as indeed there is about other portraits of the family. This could be explained by the fact that in the Fearon's home at that time, apparently working as a servant, was a man named Lamqua, himself a painter of no mean ability. It has been said[7] that it was through Lamqua's attendance on Chinnery that he was introduced to painting. However it is doubtful if he could have acquired so much knowledge and developed his technique so quickly. It would seem he had some ability as an artist even before he encountered Chinnery and that he made a careful study of Chinnery's style. The relationship between Lamqua and Chinnery will however be studied in greater depth later.

Another portrait Chinnery painted — perhaps while he waited for sitters — was of himself. This is the 1825 self-portrait which he later presented to a prominent American merchant, Benjamin Chew Wilcocks of Philadelphia.[8] Wilcocks was an old China hand and had been American Consul in Canton and perhaps Chinnery calculated that this portrait, hanging in one of the prominent homes in Macau would be the best advertisement for George Chinnery, newly arrived Vice-Regal artist from Calcutta. The self-portrait measuring 8⅝ by 7¼ inches is now in the Metropolitan Museum in New York and shows Chinnery at 51, with a "fiercer and less tolerant expression; the jowl and lips are fuller, the eyes are more penetrating, the tufted eyebrows almost Mephistophelean."[9]

Benjamin Wilcocks posed for Chinnery in 1828 and the portrait is signed and dated on the folded letter in front of an ink stand in the portrait. This painting, which is in the possession of the Hongkong and Shanghai Banking Corporation today, is one of the best from the early Macau period and shows the "High Devil", as the Chinese nicknamed the tall American, standing by his desk in the study, with a high-winged collar and cravat adding an air of distinction. Chinnery, incidentally, also favoured the high-winged collar which flared under his chin and this gave these two sartorially conscious men something in common.[10] Wilcocks was evidently a patron of artists, since he financed the studies in Europe of Thomas Sully, the renowned American portrait painter.[11]

In time, Chinnery became dependent on the patronage of a few merchants, prominent among them being William Jardine and James Matheson, who welcomed the arrival of this outstanding artist with such a brilliant record in India.[12] He soon established a place for himself among the Europeans in Macau. His eccentricities were regarded with affection and his talents rapidly became a subject of comment and admiration.

Very shortly after his arrival in Macau, Chinnery resumed sketching. He would get out at first light, set up his chair and drawing board and begin work. Harriet Low recorded in her diary in July 1833 "he gets up at 5 o'clock and goes out and makes sketches and earns his breakfast certainly." An old resident of Macau, Manuel da Silva Mendes, well-known as a teacher of Portuguese in the Lyceum in Macau, wrote on May 7, 1916 about an even older resident named Henrique Hyndman who actually remembered Chinnery.

"Perchance he is the only living one of the generation of the past century who can give direct authentic testimony regarding Chinnery. Hyndman remembers during his boyhood seeing Chinnery on the streets of Macau, having set up his work bench, with his palette and easel, depicting before the eyes of the astounded Chinese, who consider him a lunatic, the most

Two scenes from Canton, one showing a Chinese peepshow and the other is of the waterfront with a junk in the foreground and the foreign factories in the background, sketched in 1832.

picturesque spots in the city. One day passing the residence of the artist, Hyndman saw with curiosity, a candle perched in the door of the street gate. He reached out to seize it – it was painted." Others speak of a "lantern" painted on the door to his home. It was a *tromp d'oeuil* for which Chinnery was famous. He had painted, as will be recalled in D'Oyly's poem, a bunch of keys on a nail in his Calcutta studio, which intrigued many a visitor.

Chinnery was passionately interested in the world around him, sketching out of doors day after day for the sheer pleasure of recording his immediate impressions and as one critic has written[13] "his swift calligraphic pencil traces the same scenes and incidents with unflagging concentration and vitality." His sketches vary from rough pencil outlines consisting of a few strokes, to fine drawings, filled out in ink, occasionally with sepia. Sometimes he would draw a number of subjects on a single page, using both sides; in other cases he would work on a single finished drawing. Often these were accompanied by shorthand notes usually with the date. These sketches were both a means to an end – sometimes a plan or a detail for a painting in water-colours or oils – and an end in themselves.

Action was all important to Chinnery particularly the position of the body, the bend of the knee, the way a hand gripped an oar or a blacksmith's hammer, and this could only be drawn "from nature" and perfected with constant practice. On many occasions he made a number of drawings of the same action. He was clearly determined to get it right. It was not just the action, however, but the smaller details that he worked on in an attempt to achieve perfection. He would sketch an unusual pair of shoes, the elaborate design of an ornamented flower pot, the rococo detail of a church, the rigging of a junk or the queue of plaited hair worn by Chinese men in imperial China. How many thousands of drawings he made is impossible to estimate; in one major collection alone there are as many as 10,000 varying from a few rough pencil strokes to finished works of art. Many of Chinnery's illustrations were assembled into albums with contents sheets written in beautiful copperplate handwriting – a legacy of his grandfather's training – and an illustrated frontispiece showing a view with the title such as *Sketches in Macau* or *Sketches of Canton*.

A number of these albums survive, either completely or else as individual pages. One of the more frequent scenes Chinnery painted was the Praya Grande of Macau, a striking composition at any time; but by using an attractive tree or a figure sitting on a wall in the foreground looking down on to the harbour, he achieved a much more artistic effect. Among these illustrations have been found pictures of Macau's famous Church of St Paul's before a fire destroyed it in 1835 leaving only the facade, an interior scene of the British Factory in Canton with its quaint fire engine standing under the arches, and the Canton foreshore with its flotillas of junks and sampans and the beflagged foreign Factories in the background.

One of Chinnery's favourite scenes was a group of street-corner gamblers and invariably he presents us with a lively, boisterous gathering; it was obviously a common sight in Macau and Canton, as were the ubiquitous hawkers and barbers. In Chinnery's time one British visitor to Canton, the Rev. G. N. Wright, estimated there were 7,000 barbers in business, the majority operating in the street. Writing on the social habits of the Chinese, Mr Wright said that every Chinese man had to be clean-shaven until he was 40. "No beard, no moustache, nor a single hair is suffered to wander over any part of the face and thus the attendance of a barber is lastingly required," he wrote. The entire scalp was shaved to a point near the back of the skull where a queue of hair was allowed to grow and this large dome-like head is a striking feature of Chinnery's pictures. In his oils and water-colours, he sometimes achieves an impressionistic effect with the result that the male head becomes almost a caricature.

An intriguing sight in the streets of Canton was the peep-show box which was carried by itinerant hawkers. This was in the form of a model junk complete with masts. The hawker would trundle it around and for a few coppers, children could look through the portholes at the scenes inside.

Feasts and festivals, New Year gatherings, crowded market scenes as well as the stately homes of the rich merchants and the hovels of the poor: all these were subjects for Chinnery's tireless and unflagging pencil and the composite picture they offer of life in these times is lively and instructive. Animals seem particularly to have fascinated the artist and his drawings ranged from camels, goats and cows to dogs, cats and chickens. In one lively cartoon he has drawn a parrot pouring forth a torrent of abuse, and in another a cat with its back arched and its fur on end, spitting at a tormenting dog.

Chinnery seems to have derived considerable pleasure from his labours and looking through these sketches it is possible to understand why he developed such a deep attachment to Macau for he found there a peace of mind that eluded him in India and a way of life that made no demands on him.

For the first few years he was in China, Chinnery travelled up to Canton regularly during the trading season. Several writers have suggested this was prompted by fears that his wife might follow him from Calcutta. Canton was out of bounds to foreign women – although we know from Harriet Low's journal that several defied the ban and succeeded in getting ashore.

W. C. Hunter[14] tells an amusing story that when Chinnery first visited Canton he declared: "Now I am all right – what a kind providence is this Chinese Government, that it forbids the softer sex from coming and bothering us here. What an admirable arrangement, is it not?" Chinnery rolled up his eyes and added: "Laus Deo". But he was not the misogynist he would have us believe and it would seem that a far more compelling reason for his visits to Canton was the quest for commissions from European members of the Factories and from any Chinese wealthy and willing enough to sit for a portrait – for in those days many Chinese dreaded "having their likeness taken"[15] and indeed until more recent times a similar reluctance was to be found among village people in Hongkong to being photographed.

Chinnery obviously succeeded in breaking down the resistance of the Hong merchants and he picked up many other commissions during his Canton visits. He also quickly established a wide circle of friends and being a gregarious and generally cheery personality he was good company in this male and money-minded society. His jaunts to Canton provided a stimulus to his artistic palette, moreover, for, five years after his arrival in China, he began sending portraits to the Royal Academy in London, a practice he continued at intermittent intervals until 1846 when he sent his masterpiece – his own self-portrait.

The first to be shipped was of Dr Morrison engaged in translating the Bible into Chinese, a brilliant portrait that gave decided pleasure to Morrison. He wrote to Sir George Staunton, President of the Select Committee of the East India Company, on February 24, 1829 that Chinnery's painting, showing him with two Chinese colleagues at work on translation, had been much admired. "The gentlemen of the Factory have sent it home to be engraved at their expense as a token of regard and esteem for an old friend," he wrote and added that the impressions of the engraving, after the subscribers had each taken one, were to be sold for the benefit of his Anglo-Chinese College which Morrison, following his trip north to Peking with Lord Amherst in 1816, set up in Dutch-controlled Malacca in 1818.[16]

Some indication of the esteem in which Morrison was held by the East India Company can be gained from this testimony which accompanied the appeal for subscriptions for the

One of Chinnery's masterpieces in Macau showed the Rev. Dr Morrison translating the Bible into Chinese, with his two assistants. It was commissioned by members of the British factory in China in 1830 and after Chinnery finished the painting it was engraved by C. Turner, A.R.A. in London. This engraving carries the following inscription: To the Rev Dr Morrison this portrait of himself engaged in translating the Bible in the Chinese language is dedicated in unanimous testimony of that regard by the makers of the British factory in China. Published March 29, 1830.

engraving: "Mr Chinnery has just finished a most excellent picture of Dr Morrison, attended by two Chinese teachers. If Dr Morrison will consent to sacrifice, for the space of one year, the gratification which he must necessarily derive from the possession of this portrait to the wishes of his friends . . . it is proposed to request him to allow this picture to be sent to England, in the *Orwell*, for the purpose of obtaining from it the most perfect mezzotinto engraving that can be taken. The celebrated artist to whom they are indebted for this portrait of Dr Morrison, has expressed his readiness to undertake the commission of procuring the engraving. These gentlemen who wish to testify this mark of esteem and respect for Dr Morrison are requested to affix their signatures." This engraving was subsequently made in London at a cost of 300 guineas.

Morrison replied: "Permit me to request you to make known to them the grateful sense which I entertain of the kind spirit which induced so favourable a testimony, after about 22 years' residence in China. This expression of goodwill from the members of the Hon. Company's Factory affords real satisfaction to an old servant. As Mr Chinnery has taken the utmost pains with this picture, and produced a painting which is I believe, gratifying as a work of art to all who have seen it, instead of accepting more than a few copies of the engraving I would resign those you suggested appropriating to me, to Mr Chinnery's disposal."

This was typical of Morrison's selflessness. One historian[17] has said that "this intense man of piety and prayer, a fearless preacher and prophet, must have been an outstanding and arresting public figure in the Canton-Macau community of his day; he shunned the effervescence of the social life of the times as a total abstainer would shun champagne; when his family were with him he could often be seen enjoying his daily romp with the children during their evening relaxation in front of his house; but when they were home in England, he led the life of a recluse, cloistered with his books and his teachers, his disciples and his God."

Morrison died five years later, having shortly before accepted the appointment of Chinese Secretary and Interpreter to Lord Napier who had just arrived to take up the post of Chief Superintendent of Trade at Canton, following the ending of the East India Company's monopoly.

Shortly after the Morrison portrait, Chinnery sent another of a Hong merchant to the Royal Academy and a year later four more including one of Howqua who had played a prominent part in Sino-western trade and indeed was regarded as a legendary figure among the western merchants in Canton. It may be wondered why Chinnery chose to send the Hong merchant portraits to the Academy. There was obviously more to them than just their colourful robes and their novel oriental setting which might excite the people of London.

Chinnery had obviously heard much about them and had come to admire them for the exacting and difficult role they occupied in relation to the western traders. He must have heard stories about their vast fortunes, their probity as businessmen and the huge squeeze they often had to pay to Chinese officialdom. Their fame had travelled to England and the image of Howqua was in later years to be made in wax and exhibited at Madame Tussaud's, ranking second only to the popular figure of the Duke of Wellington.[18]

In 1720, five years after the East India Company had established itself at Canton as the principal European agency trading with China, the Hong merchants formed themselves into a body corporate. Collectively they were known as the Co-Hong and they were, with the exception of the year 1725, the monopolists of the foreign trade who dealt with the 'barbarians' from the west.

The family from which Howqua descended became associated with the Co-Hong in the

An oil portrait by Chinnery in his Macau period shows this unidentified man with his dog.

— Courtesy Hongkong and Shanghai Banking Corpn

year 1731 when the first Howqua, named Wu Kuo-ying, obtained the appointment. Three further Howquas were active at later times, including Howqua II, the third son of the first Howqua and named Wu Ping-chien, who was the subject of Chinnery's painting. The name Howqua was obviously a family business name which was handed down from father to son.

Apart from carrying on business — and this was the sweeter and highly lucrative side of their job — they would receive all complaints or petitions addressed to the local authorities — and this proved an increasingly difficult task.

They were in fact the middle men appointed by China to act as go-betweens in all matters between the foreign traders and Chinese officialdom. At the same time strict regulations governed the activities of foreigners who were allowed to reside in Canton only between September and March and on condition that they did not bring their wives and families with them.

In 1825, when Chinnery arrived in China, the principal Hong merchants were Howqua, Mowqua, Pwankeiqua, Pwansuylan, Chunqua, Kingqua and Gouqua — the "qua" being a title for an official — and the Co-Hong was limited to 13.

They obtained their position through the payment of large sums of money at Peking — as much as £55,000 — for what was in effect a franchise, and a contemporary writer, W. C. Hunter, [19] tells us that "if the licence thus acquired was costly, it secured to them uninterrupted and extraordinary pecuniary advantage. But on the other hand it subjected them to calls or 'squeezes' for contributions to public works or buildings, for the relief of districts suffering from a scarcity of rice, as well as for the often imaginary and over-estimated damage caused by the overflowing of the Yangtze River."

The same writer tells of a conversation with Howqua, who was the Hong merchant to several British and American firms in Canton.

"Well, Howqua, what news have you got today?"

"Have got too muchee bad news," he replied. "Hwang Ho (the river) have spilum too muchee."

"Man-te-le (pidgin for Mandarin) have come to see you?"

"He no come see my, he sendee come one piece 'chop'. He come to-mollo. He wantchee my two-lac dollar."

"You pay he how muchee," asked Hunter, who by the way spoke fluent Cantonese.

"My pay he fitty, sikky tousand so," came the reply.

"But s'pose he no contentee?"

"S'pose he No 1 no contentee, my pay he one lac."

This dialogue illustrated the sort of demands made upon the senior Hong merchants who knew they were being squeezed and that the money was going not to flood relief but to fatten the pockets of venal provincial officials.

In 1841 just before the British forces were about to launch an attack on Canton, it was called off at the last moment when the city consented to pay a ransom of $2 million and again the Hong merchants bore the brunt of that ransom, Howqua himself paying $1.1 million and the rest paying another $900,000 between them.

It is interesting to read how Howqua justified his tremendous contribution which he acknowledged was a concession to fung shui. He apportioned his donation this way: $800,000 in recognition of his own prosperity, $200,000 because of the unswerving filial piety of his eldest son and $100,000 for his youngest son who happened to be born when Howqua reached the age of 60 – a very happy omen.

This diversion was necessary to illustrate the very real affection in which the Hong merchants were held by the foreign traders in Canton. The portrait of Howqua, ranks as Chinnery's finest. Another outstanding painting was Chinnery's picture of Mowqua and in both pictures there is a feast of detail and colour for the eye to linger on. Both are today in the possession of the Hongkong and Shanghai Banking Corporation.

Chinnery's original portrait of Howqua was painted for Hon W. H. Chicheley Plowden, an agent of the East India Company and resident in the British Factory in Canton who returned to England in 1834. Chinnery could, no doubt, have made a small fortune painting copies of the portraits of the Hong merchants but if the tempting thought ever occurred to him he resisted it. Others however jumped on the Chinnery bandwagon and partly at the request of merchants who wanted copies to hang in their offices and homes or to be sent to their principals overseas, a flourishing business sprang up among Chinese painters copying the Chinnery originals. These copies have turned up all over the world and a critic who has made a study of those found in various museums in the United States[20] has said that "the faces in all these portraits differ widely from the Hongkong portrait. Possibly this lack of definite resemblance is due to the carelessness of the copyists, but there is also to be considered the possibility that all these Chinese copies are stylised in the Chinese manner into what might be called 'a Hong merchant type' representing a sort of symbolic likeness of Howqua II".

He adds: "It is obvious that the Hongkong Chinnery is the only portrait of Howqua that may be said to have been painted in a truly accomplished western manner such as one would expect from the brush of Chinnery. The other portraits of Howqua, in spite of their long-standing attribution to Chinnery, almost without exception speak of western art with a strong Cantonese accent."

Who were these Chinese painters who copied Chinnery's masterpieces? One was Lamqua and his relationship with Chinnery forms the subject of the next chapter.

9

Chinnery's great rival

CHINNERY's opinion of his own work was certainly not coloured with false modesty. He had written to his pupil, Mrs Browne, in Calcutta that "there are not 6 at home even who I would stand in any awe of" and there is little dispute that in both India and Macau he was one of the best western painters to have lived there. Yet repeatedly in his Macau years Chinnery found himself at odds with a Chinese artist whose talents he scarcely acknowledged. This was the man named Lamqua.

How he got this strange alias is not known for his real name was Kwan Kiu-chin. Lam may have been a family name and the word *qua* (or *Kuan*, in Mandarin, or *Koon* in Cantonese) is shown in Chinese dictionaries to mean either "an official" or "a term of respect". In the case of painters like Lamqua, the second meaning appears more likely.

Lamqua's first encounter with Chinnery was apparently in his early years in Macau when he stayed with the Fearon family and when Lamqua was said to have been a servant there.[1] It is widely believed that he was Chinnery's pupil though with Lamqua's faltering pidgin English and Chinnery's limited knowledge of Chinese it is difficult to understand how they could have communicated effectively. More likely is it that Lamqua, already a passable painter, watched Chinnery at work and picked up some of his techniques for he seems to have been a highly intelligent and perceptive person. To have built up his business within a few years and to have dominated the native artists in Macau, Canton and later Hongkong, indicates a talent that goes well beyond even the amateur levels that Chinnery encountered among his friends in India.

Certainly it is difficult to imagine Lamqua as no more than a servile flunkey standing in the background cleaning the great man's paint-brushes. Lamqua has been quoted as saying that he had been a favourite pupil and an assistant of the 'foreign devil' but had repudiated his tutelage.[2] It was not long before Lamqua, in addition to setting up his own studio in Canton, was submitting pictures for international exhibition and these were accepted by the Royal Academy in London twice within a space of ten years – the head of an old man in 1835, and Capt. W. H. Hall of the East India Company paddle-steamer *Nemesis* in 1845. In 1841 he exhibited in the Apollo Club in New York, ten years later in the Pennsylvania Academy of Fine Arts, again at the Boston Athenaeum and again in 1860 in the Pennsylvania Academy. If as Chinnery claims he never taught Lamqua[3] then the Chinese artist is all the more deserving of admiration for his talent and skill.

It would of course be an exaggeration to rank him with Chinnery either as an artist or draughtsman, but one writer[4] says of his portraits that "they are some of the most impressive paints (in the English style) executed for the western market." Nor does he appear to have had

Chinnery's talent for sketching. As a businessman, however, he was incomparably better and he set up a studio in Canton which, from a number of contemporary reports, seems to have had a prodigious output. There he employed upwards of 20 assistants and they catered largely for the tourist trade. These paintings were generally much inferior to Lamqua's own work, but the prices were also considerably lower than Chinnery's – generally about one-fifth.[5] It was not only the price that proved attractive to tourists, however, but the novelty of having a painting done by a Chinese artist.

Lamqua's portraits, however, were not a gimmicky souvenir unlikely to last longer than the trip home. Many discerning visitors to Canton and Macau spoke highly of his work and not a few referred to him as the "Sir Thomas Lawrence of China". Henry Charles Sirr, an author and visitor to Macau and Canton described him as the Sir Thomas Lawrence and Hogarth of China – "and he well deserves this proud distinction."[6]

Not only was Lamqua an accomplished artist, as one can see from his self-portrait bought for Hongkong's City Museum and Art Gallery, but he entertained his customers with unflagging enthusiasm and invited many to roam over his three-storey studio which consisted of the ground-floor shop with its well-stocked counters, the main workroom on the first floor and his own private studio at the top. Tourists would watch his assistants with their long queues tied around the backs of their heads, working on rice-paper paintings or pictures on glass.

A French visitor to Canton in 1849-50[7] readily acknowledged that in this side of Lamqua's business there was no art. "It is a purely mechanical operation in which the system of division of labour is faithfully practised. One painter makes trees all his life – another figures; this one draws feet and hands – that one houses. Thus each acquires in his line a certain perfection, particularly in the finish of details, but none of them is capable of undertaking an entire painting. Lamqua may really pass for an artist; his pupils are scarcely better than workmen."

Lamqua was not only interested in the tourist trade but catered to Chinese customers as well[8] and several visitors tell of the many pictures they saw in his studio of the reigning Emperor, Tao Kwang, and the Goddess of Mercy, Kwan Yin, while his native artists also produced other traditional paintings admired by Chinese people including flowers, trees, landscapes and birds. As for the quality, many of the portraits "were excellent likenesses and though deficient in light and shade, were executed in a most masterly manner."[9] This observation was fairly typical. Another said that "the greatest defect which we notice in examining the state of the art in this distant country, and which is most repugnant of our notions of propriety, is the total ignorance of the artist with regard to the effect of light and shade. Accordingly we find that from the want of this essential every object looks meagre, and without the roundness or prominence which is often required."[10]

However the visitors paid tribute to the invariably "excellent" colouring they found in Chinese paintings and they were particularly struck by the copies which Chinese artists in general could make of a European work of art.

Lamqua's studios were thus well patronised by visitors and if lower prices, the sheer novelty of a Chinese painting and a surprisingly high quality portrait were not enough, Lamqua proved to be as much a character as Chinnery himself.

His shop carried signs such as "Lamqua: English and Chinese painter" and "Lamqua, handsome face painter" which were eye-catchers for the visiting British or American sailor or tourist. Lamqua himself, though limited in his vocabulary, earned many a chuckle for his shrewd and adroit observations in English. He is credited[11] with having said to a

This self-portrait of the Chinese artist Lamqua, Chinnery's rival in his Macau days, was painted in about 1854. It was acquired by the Hongkong Government and is now part of the collection of the City Museum and Art Gallery.

These two views show the facade of Macau's famous landmark of St Paul's, destroyed by fire shortly after this sketch was made in 1834, and below, the ruins of the church after the fire.

— Courtesy Victoria and Albert Museum

76

disgruntled client "How can handsome face make, when handsome face no got?"

To another visitor[12] he condemned a local "English belle" by saying "her face is too round, she has colour in her cheeks, her eyes are too blue; she's too tall, too plump – yi-yaw – her face talks and she has feet so large that she can walk on them." This must have been translated for the visitor, for Lamqua later inveighs against the errors that western artists made in their drawings of Chinese scenes in fluent pidgin: "suppose English man know plenty, why for talk lie pigeon all some dat; me tink he plenty foolo; Chinaman no all same foolo, what see can do, what no see no can do."

Little wonder the visitors to Canton made a point of calling at his studio. Little wonder they invariably spoke glowingly of his ability. He played up to his gallery well by inviting them to watch him at work and his showmanship paid dividends in the business it brought him.

It would seem that many of the tributes showered on Lamqua were reported back to Chinnery though whether he felt a real and permanent sense of grievance or, good actor that he was, played his part in creating a legend, he invariably responded with indignation, denying Lamqua was his pupil. One visitor[13] said "He was a little disturbed by any casual allusion to his brother of the brush – Lamqua."

Another visitor[14] reports that "between these two men exists a rivalry that is all the more lively due to the fact that they lived together. To hear Chinnery talk, Lamqua is a subaltern, a wretchedly bad painter whose sole merit comes from having stolen from him some models and some methods. To hear Lamqua talk, he was the favourite student and assistant to the English painter. Chinnery whose talent is far superior to that of Lamqua asks 50 to 100 piastres for the same portrait that the native artist makes for 15 to 20; and because they are cheaper, untutored people frequently prefer to give their business to Lamqua; whence the hatred."

Another writer[15] claimed that the name of Lamqua used to excite Chinnery to "uncontrolled fury." Certainly the charges of copying were well-founded. An American sea captain, Robert Bennet Forbes tells us that he took his portrait by Chinnery to be copied by Lamqua.[16] And while it is not certain who copied Chinnery's famous painting of the Hong merchant Howqua, it is believed he sat only once for the British artist and there is no evidence that Chinnery ever made any copies. Lamqua could have been responsible for some of them.

However, he painted from life as well, and one of his notable pictures done in the Chinnery manner is of Dr Peter Parker sitting in his surgery in Canton (with a Factory flag billowing outside the window) while his Chinese pupil examines a patient's eye. The Chinese pupil is said to be Lamqua's nephew, Kwan A-to[17] which if true suggests the Kwans were a talented family for Lamqua's younger brother was the artist, Tingqua, who in addition to being a miniaturist was to become one of the most important Chinese water-colourists in the western style.[18]

The association with Dr Parker led to commissions to paint a large number of portraits of his patients in the Canton hospital and in the Yale Medical Library in the U.S. are 86 of these paintings while at Guy's Hospital, London are another 23 showing people suffering from various diseases or with amputations. A further painting is at Countway Library, Boston, making 110 in all. These somewhat gruesome paintings "provide a startling insight into the painter's ability and style. Some reach the heights of the finest English portraiture as represented by Sir Thomas Lawrence or Sir William Beechey."[19]

Lamqua painted these pictures for Dr Parker free of charge as a way of expressing thanks for the work of the American medical missionary. The paintings are not only noteworthy for

Two of Chinnery's early sketches in Macau and Canton. The upper picture shows part of the Citadel and Franciscan Fort, drawn on December 10, 1825 about 10 weeks after his arrival in Macau. The lower picture shows the American factory in Canton drawn in 1826.

their artistic quality, but particularly valuable as medical records for as one writer has noted "they usually focus on documenting gross pathology, especially tumours of a maturity (commonly five to 30 years) only rarely witnessed by Western surgeons today." Moreover about half the paintings are of special interest because Dr Parker's case descriptions have survived, and can be corelated with the portraits.[20]

Admittedly because of his nephew's professional association with Dr Parker, Lamqua was the logical choice to paint these often horrifying deformities; the fact that he did them with such care and faithfulness despite his busy commercial workload testifies to a generous and compassionate nature which the petty rivalry with Chinnery tends to obscure.

* * *

In 1835 when Chinnery was still a highly fashionable portraitist in Macau, he was hailed by the Canton Register in these terms: "This gentleman should be ordered home by the ladies of the land in the UK for we can assure them now that they have lost Sir Thomas Lawrence they will never again look so beautiful unless under the *vivida vis* of the sparkling and magic touch of Chinnery. The knighthood would then follow as a matter of course, as having been most deservedly earned and richly merited." Yet the Register went on to pay handsome compliments to Lamqua and said "we can assure our readers that if they wish to live — if not everlastingly yet for a very respectable number of the periods of the revolutions in his orbit of our late cometic visitor that they cannot do better — or doubtless in all cases, make a more handsome or acceptable memorial to their mothers, sisters, their fair lady's loves, or even to their best friends, their wives, than their own sweet countenances, drawn by Lamqua, whose charge is . . . $ 15 for a rare facsimile."

If Chinnery was not feeling the hot breath of competition at that stage it certainly grew with the years and as Lamqua gained fame, Chinnery's output of portraits in oil, which had earned him a fortune in his India days and continued to keep him active in his early Macau years, began to dwindle.

While Chinnery was able to prove that he could still have his paintings hung in the Royal Academy, Lamqua also showed he was good enough to be accorded the same privilege and his paintings were additionally exhibited in Paris and in the United States.

Lamqua was not the only local artist to have been influenced by Chinnery. A more direct link is said to have existed between Chinnery and Marciano Baptista[21] who was described as "incomparably superior" to his Chinese colleague. Baptista is reported to have worked as Chinnery's assistant at one time where he helped grind colours; in return Chinnery encouraged him with his drawing and helped to develop his technique. His drawings, like D'Oyly's in India, bear the strong imprint of Chinnery's teaching.

There were others with names like Protinqua, Sinqua, Yeuqua, Chingqua, Chowqua, Lai Sung, Hin Qua and Yam Qua but an eminent scholar of China trade paintings[22] has said "apart from Lamqua, the rest are largely stencil or stretcher label identifications whose names are pidgin English and whose connections with Chinnery are nebulous."

People who bought their work were for the most part not interested in great masterpieces but simply a lively souvenir and these paintings still possess interesting historical associations and sometimes an undeniable period charm.[23]

One thing Lamqua's contemporaries did not know was how to paint portraits that would survive and here Chinnery scored. The makeshift canvases used by many Chinese artists did not stand up well to the passage of time and some today are split and rotted at the edges.[24] While Chinnery and his Chinese contemporaries probably used the same pigments, the Chinese copyists seem to have used some oil or varnish (perhaps lacquer) in mixing their colours and these have caused their pictures to crackle and wrinkle on the paint surface.

A French visitor to Lamqua's studio said the Chinese colours were much inferior to the European. They scarcely succeeded in manufacturing any beside vermilion, lazulite, carmine and orpiment, and "the best painters, especially portrait painters buy other paints of the English."[25] Chinnery was careful about the quality of paints he used, which he ground and mixed in his own studio, and took particular care in preparing his paintings for export.

Today while Chinnery's paintings grace the (mainly private) walls of commercial institutions, public buildings and art galleries in various parts of the world, Lamqua's survive largely for historical reasons and because they have acquired a certain curiosity value though their merit in many cases cannot be denied.

Their rivalry, though doubtless real at the time, seems from this distance petty and exaggerated. That Chinnery could not manage to earn as much in his later years in Macau as in his earlier years or during his time in Calcutta was partly due to Lamqua's prices but also to the exodus of foreigners from Macau after 1839 and the artist's increasing preference for sketching and possibly also a decline in activity with advancing years.

Also it should not be forgotten that when his output in oils dwindled he produced one of his finest portraits — his self-portrait — which demonstrated his superiority over all other artists in the region and this was Chinnery's most convincing way of showing it.

10

The women in his life

IT is tempting to see all the women in Chinnery's life in terms of romantic attachments and after his known affairs and dalliances in India the suspicion arises that in Macau his interest in Assor, the Tanka sampan girl and Harriet Low, the niece of an American business-man, was more than the professional interest of an artist in his sitter.

The record – certainly in the case of Harriet Low – proves otherwise. It will be recalled Chinnery took a mistress in Calcutta by whom he had two sons. It would not be unreasonable to suppose that with his discerning eye for a pretty face and young figure he would have found Harriet a pleasant companion and Assor, a charming model.

Clearly, Chinnery spent much time with Harriet both painting her very attractive portrait and later coaching and encouraging her in her artistic inclinations. Remembering the Mrs Browne affair in Calcutta, it is tempting to conclude that the same sort of infatuation developed between Chinnery and Harriet. The American girl obviously enjoyed his company.

Her journal[1] records that on April 2, 1833 she "went to that amusing man, Chinnery, and stayed till after two sketching. There is a good deal to be gathered from his conversation and some of his similes are most amusing. He has been a great observer of human nature, for which he has had every opportunity, his profession having brought him in contact with people of high and low degree. He has been in Calcutta and has seen a great variety of characters, as you may suppose, in that changing place. He has excellent sense, and plumes himself upon being 'though not handsome, excessively genteel'; his personal appearance, I think, however is rather against him, for he is what I call fascinatingly ugly, and what with a habit he has of distorting his features in a most un-Christian manner, and with taking snuff, smoking and snorting, I think, were he not so agreeable, he would be intolerable. But, to give him his due, he is really polite, and speaks well of everyone. Being one of his special favourites, I must say something for him; to use his own expression, he 'buckles' to me. We were asking him if Afun (in the portrait Chinnery was painting of Dr Thomas R. Colledge) could keep still enough to be painted. 'Ma'am,' he said, 'the Rock of Gibraltar is calves'-foot jelly to him'."

Just a few days earlier she had described him as "a droll genius – a most amusing man of very good information and good sense" and she discovered a little later that "he has a face made on purpose to tell stories."

Harriet is a fascinating girl but she came from a strait-laced family in Salem, Massachusetts, was a keen student of the Bible and as has been noted, read sermons on Sunday if she could not attend church; scholars are emphatic that she had no romantic illusions about Chinnery.[2] Harriet was indeed attracted to Dr Colledge who distinguished himself as a surgeon in Canton and Macau, particularly in the treatment of diseases of the eye.

These two sitters are unnamed and unknown. The shorthand at the foot of the upper sketch reads: "It ought to be the other leg up and the lower part of the figure turned this way. November 9, '47".

— Courtesy Victoria and Albert Museum, London

82

Writing of Dr Colledge after a two-hour visit to her home in March 1832 she said "He is a 'darling', the best Englishman I ever saw. He is truly good at heart. I believe there is no nonsense about him" – high praise indeed remembering her castigation of the young Englishmen of Macau.

If she harboured hopes of marrying Dr Colledge, however, these were to be dashed when her friend and former schoolmate from Salem, Caroline Matilda Shillaber, who arrived in Macau in December, 1831, fell in love with the young doctor and married him two years later.

Quite apart from Harriet Low's interest in Dr Colledge she in turn was being courted by two men in Macau, one the Rev. G. H. Vachell of the East India Company, and the other, W. W. Wood, a young American who sketched and possibly studied under Chinnery at one time, for the Cooper Union Museum acquired some years ago an album of drawings by Chinnery covering the early period of his life in Macau, which contained a frontispiece drawn by Wood entitled *Sketches in China*.

Wood, who was one of Chinnery's close friends, made a reputation for himself by editing the first English-language newspaper in China, the Canton Register. He was also its compositor and his foolscap-size paper was printed on a handpress lent by Alexander Matheson, the leading British merchant. But he was not favoured by Harriet's uncle and guardian. After working in Canton he went to Manila, but never married.[3] Harriet records in her journal her meetings and feelings about both Vachell and Wood though identifies them only by their initials, and while the affair with Wood seemed at one stage promising, in her final year Harriet became disillusioned and harsh and she wrote in her diary after receiving a letter from him in Canton, "I feel my heart grows harder every day and I am perfectly astonished when I think how differently I view all that has passed from what I did a few months since, and wonder what has produced this change."

Before Harriet left Macau in November, 1833, however, she had her portrait painted by Chinnery and she records in her diary "I am to have my phiz. painted, great presumption on my part, I think, but it was the request of Uncle and Aunt, and the thought of the pleasure it would give you all that induced me. I sat for an hour, looking at one of the ugliest men in existence, but he makes himself so agreeable that you quite forget how ugly he is. He requested me to have the mouth open, a thing which I abominate in a picture, but he says it will never do to have it shut, as I generally keep it a little open.

"Well there I sat, with my head screwed and twisted in a strange manner till after he had finished the first sketch and then I looked at it. O ye powers, what a thing! and yet I think it must be like me, because I saw mother's look about the eyes, also Cousin Forster's whom I was always said to resemble, but such a fright! I have laughed fifty-one times since, to think of it. The head appears about ready to take leave of the neck, the mouth is open as though I were snoring; there is a little something yclept nose, and a place where the eyes should be. I suppose I must wait with patience for a few more sittings, but I think it will rather lower my vanity." This first sketch on April 9 was followed by another entry on April 15. "I went to Chinnery's and looked at the man till two, when I found myself in a better humour with my portrait, which will, I think, be an excellent likeness, and a little paint will make it better-looking than I am, I fear. You can make allowances for the paint. Chinnery said some good things, and we passed the morning very pleasantly."

Again later: "I sat three hours – he has made a little alteration – put a book in the hand and I like it much better."

On May 10 there was another sitting when Harriet went to have "my face painted. Sat

These two ink sketches show a beggar in a Macau street, and a child watching two swayback pigs eating. The + mark shown at the foot of the page indicates it was drawn roughly at first and the circle with the dot inside indicates that Chinnery completed or "filled in" the drawing in ink at a later date. The date is illegible.

— Courtesy Hongkong and Shanghai Banking Corpn

This picture shows a man wearing the cangue, a form of punishment for minor misdemeanours imposed by Chinese magistrates.

— Courtesy Victoria and Albert Museum

Chinnery's pen sketches of life in Macau provide some of the most endearing mementos of a bygone age. The street gamblers in the above picture attract the baleful stare of a resting dog. Today this ancient custom has been institutionalised in the form of casinos which are well patronised day and night not only by local people but tourists as well. The upper picture shows a man eating a bowl of noodles from a street stall.

— Courtesy of the Hongkong and Shanghai Banking Corpn.

with all the patience I could muster from eleven to three, in hopes it would be the last sitting but there is one more to come. The room is so hot that it is almost insupportable, not a breath of air from out-of-doors is allowed to enter, but I have the one satisfaction that the picture must give you pleasure, for the likeness is said by everyone to be perfect. They say I have run against the canvas and left my impression there, so the thought consoles me for all the exertion I make in this hot weather.''

Five days later she went for her last sitting and Harriet wrote: "The likeness is said to be perfect, but I think it is a very ugly face. It has not raised my vanity in the least. I sat there till nearly three, when I was quite exhausted, and very glad to leave the 'studio'.''

When it was finished the picture justifiably won high praise and Harriet writes of friends coming to see it. They "say it is to the life, so does everyone, and I only hope you will think so too.''

She wrote of other visits to Chinnery's but clearly the ordeal of the sitting had diminished her interest but while she "drew a little" she added that "I do not take the same interest in the amusement as I did last year, the change of masters makes a great difference, I find.'' The identity of the earlier master was not revealed. Harriet did not give up her lessons entirely for in July she wrote Chinnery a note "and gave him a little 'soft soap' (for flattery is a thing, he says, 'he cuts mutton-chops out of') and returned his sketch book, hinting that I should like another. Whether the 'soft soap' had a good effect, or what other motive he may have had, I cannot say, but in about half an hour he came himself, with another book. We had given orders 'no could see' so asked him to tea.''

There were doubtless other meetings between Chinnery and Harriet but later that year her uncle, Mr Low, was taken ill and was advised by Dr Colledge to return to America. On November 16, 1833, "Mr Chinnery called to bid us good-bye" and the Lows left Macau for good. William Low never reached the United States. He died on March 22, 1834 at Capetown. His portrait by Chinnery, painted in Macau in May, 1833, survives in a private collection in the United States.

So much for Harriet Low.

As for the two sampan girls, Assor and Alloy, there is no evidence that they were anything more than attractive models whom he painted not once but many times, and it can well be imagined that this sort of picture would have had a high souvenir value among the foreign residents of, and visitors to Macau and Canton. Chinnery, however, painted them in a number of poses. His best-known portrait shows Assor seated with her legs crossed and a big wicker fisherman's hat at her side. Behind her is a sampan hauled up on the stocks, probably her home. A junk sails in the background. She is young, attractive and on her full red lips, which Chinnery has deepened with his favourite vermilion, is an impish smile. The picture is a delightful composition which is now widely admired as one of his finest and most famous and which was exhibited at the Royal Academy in 1844. Her dainty, slim hands do not look like those of a sampan girl though her right foot is relatively big and bony and does look more like that of a girl who spends much of her time standing in the stern of a boat, working a large oar on a steel pivot such as can be seen along the China coast to this day. These were apparently the girls who rowed Chinnery and others around the harbour from time to time and from the beach to the waiting ships.

In the days of the Canton Factories, many sampan girls operated as part-time prostitutes to the sailors of naval and merchant ships.[4] Sampans or "wash boats" manned by three or four girls would pull alongside a newly arrived ship. One would call out: "Ah you missee

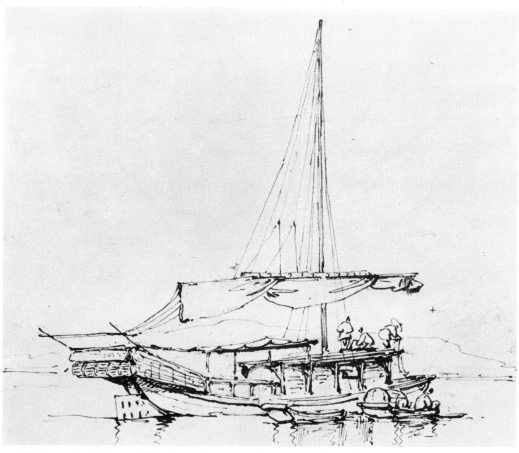

Chinnery's pictures of junks are among the most admired. He had ample opportunity to sketch them during his river trips to Canton, and from the many vantage points of Macau. Some boat people lived afloat while others pulled their sampans ashore and turned them into a home.

— Courtesy Hongkong and Shanghai Banking Corpn

While mother sits and waits with the children (above) father has his ears cleaned (below) in these two ink drawings by Chinnery.

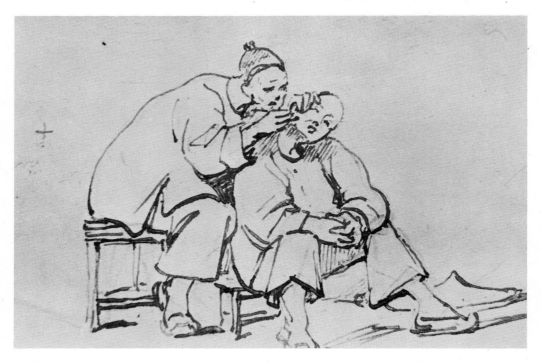

chiefee mate, how you dooa? I saavez him werry wen. You saavez my? I makee mendee, all same you shirtee last time." The sailors were delighted to see them and they were ready to be anyone's sweet-heart. [5]

However, those who have made a careful study of known Chinnery material can find no substance to the belief expressed by the authors of a book [6] that the sampan girls were his mistresses. Although many writers try to weave a romance around him, there is no evidence of his having had affairs of that kind in Macau, whatever he did in Calcutta. The belief is that he could not have endured in that strict society, much less maintained his connections with the East India Company hierarchy if there had been a breath of scandal. [7] Chinnery was after all entirely dependent on their goodwill for his business and for permission to travel to Canton – his final refuge in case his wife ever tried to follow him. Having said all this, however, it is impossible to be dogmatic about an aspect of his life on which there is no information whatever.

That Chinnery still had an eye for a trim figure is not doubted. For while there is no evidence that he ever painted an oil of a nude, there is a sketch by him in the Victoria and Albert Museum of a European woman nude from the waist up and, on the same sheet, another of the same person holding a filmy veil which barely covers her plump but pretty figure. This was apparently drawn in his Macau days but her identity is a mystery; indeed it is impossible to tell whether he drew her from life or whether he was copying a picture. Another sketch of the back view of a nude turns out to be a statue. Apart from these pencil drawings, all Chinnery's known paintings of women were formal portraits and invariably they were attired in their Sunday best.

The only other woman in his life was the one he did his best to keep out of it, but whom he continued to support. His wife incidentally, was the subject of a good many false alarms though these were possibly puckish inventions on Chinnery's part to amuse his friends and titillate his companions at dinner. He was also ever-ready to denounce her ugliness. He once told Harriet Low's aunt: "Her beauty even surpasses my own" and Mrs John Davis, wife of the last chief of the East India Company's Select Committee and later Superintendent of Trade, heard him comment: "Mrs Chinnery's appearances cannot be exaggerated. She was an ugly woman 30 years ago; what in the name of Graces must she be now." He also once told a friend that he always kept a trunk ready packed "with which to fly to Canton in case my Thalia should try to surprise me." [8]

Once or twice he did skip off to Canton at short notice, and returned when the scare was over and on another occasion when apparently Mrs Chinnery had booked passage to Macau but had to give up her cabin at the last moment to a merchant who had priority, Chinnery greeted the man with this comment: "Your hand my good fellow; you have played a card I shall never forget. You'll breakfast with me tomorrow, grateful thanks for the immense and never-to-be-forgotten service you have rendered me. Chin-chin and good luck to you; may your shadow never grow less and your Patna yield you 1,000 per cent."

As W. C. Hunter said: "There was something quite refreshing in such amusing episodes of a married life; the treatment of his own by Chinnery was as rich as a play." [9]

Two observations are necessary here. The first is that Chinnery enjoyed being the centre of attention and in fact fancied himself as an amateur actor, having played in more than one role in his Macau days and having also acted in India. It was thus Chinnery the Thespian throwing out a well-acted line to earn an easy laugh, as he so often did during his life. Behind this outward gaiety we can at times detect a more dutiful and responsible person, even if only fleetingly. Mr Geoffrey Bonsall who has made a careful study of Chinnery's shorthand, has found a note on one drawing saying "April 6, 1838. Married 40 years this day." Admittedly Chinnery had a good memory for anniversaries – in the same year he noted in shorthand that he had arrived in Madras "36 years ago this day, December 22" and elsewhere that he arrived in Dublin 42 years ago – but it would seem that there were some memories of the past which he cherished. It is perhaps Chinnery's tragedy that he could never reconcile his own personal and family life with his more overpowering impulse to paint and sketch. The only way to give free rein to one was the total exclusion of the other.

It is worthwhile nailing one myth at this point. Whether it was her inability to get a passage to Macau or Mrs Chinnery's very good sense, she did not come out to China at any time. The authors of a recent book on Chinnery[10] have repeated the fallacy that "she did in fact follow him to Canton but when she attempted to land she was not permitted to do so and was obliged to stay aboard ship where she caught smallpox and died." The truth is more prosaic. Mrs Chinnery died at the age of 88 in Brighton on December 23, 1865, of "natural decay."[11]

Assor, the sampan girl

— Courtesy Hongkong and Shanghai Banking Corpn

The Hong merchant, Howqua

— Courtesy Hongkong and Shanghai Banking Corpn

Benjamin Chew Wilcocks

The Hong merchant, Mowqua

— Courtesy Hongkong and Shanghai Banking Corpn

The Praya Grande, Macau

— Courtesy City Museum and Art Gallery, Hongkong

11

Ten portraits

CHINNERY continued to send portraits to the Royal Academy in the 1830s. One was of Mr (later Sir) John F. Davis, who had come to Canton in 1813 in the East India Company's service, accompanied the Amherst mission to Peking in 1816 and had risen to become Chairman of the Select Committee of the East India Company; then when its monopoly was abolished he became Second Superintendent of Trade under Lord Napier and on the latter's death succeeded him as Chief Superintendent. He later became Hongkong's second Governor in 1844.

Poor Davis never quite recovered from the shock of experiencing the East India Company's dissolution. He was Chief Superintendent of Trade for only three months and found he had too little power to control "the ill-conduct of the British subjects in China," and gave up "in despair". Nor did he find the British residents of Hongkong any easier to deal with when he became Governor. Six months after arriving in the colony he was writing to Lord Stanley in London that "it is a much easier task to govern the 20,000 Chinese inhabitants, than the few hundreds of English." However, he persevered with this thankless task until 1848.

A practical illustration of the recalcitrance of the English residents was their refusal to accept Davis's tax on the consumption of wines and spirits and every member of the Legislative Council, all of whom were Officials incidentally, voted against it.[1]

In 1835, a year after the Davis portrait, Chinnery sent in his picture of Lieutenant James Holman, RN, known as "The Blind Traveller", who visited Macau in 1830 after the ever-suspicious Russians had hustled him out of Siberia because, despite his blindness, they were convinced he was spying in forbidden areas. While in Macau, the adventurous Holman tried an opium pipe at the home of William Jardine – an experience which he recalls, gave him a violent headache.[2]

After Holman, came the portrait of the Rev. Charles Gutzlaff, the German missionary from Pomerania, whom Chinnery painted dressed as a Fukien sailor in which disguise he travelled to different parts in China. Besides preaching Christianity, he was a doctor. He was described by one acquaintance as "a short square figure with clothes that for shape might have been cut in his native Pomerania ages ago, a broad-brimmed straw hat, his great face beneath, with a sinister eye."[3] A pencil portrait which survives in the Peabody Museum, Salem, however, shows him with a turban or cloth tied round his head rather than a straw hat. Shorthand notes at the top of this picture say: "Mr Gutzlaff in the dress of a Fukien sailor. For Mr Lindsay September 27, 1832. Fix."

He spoke Chinese fluently and wrote it as well and had mastered several dialects. This

Chinnery's sketch of the well-known German missionary, Charles Gutzlaff, in the clothes of a Fukien sailor — a costume he wore on his visits to ports on the coast of central and north China, distributing religious tracts and on some occasions acting as interpreter for opium traders. Gutzlaff was a fluent linguist and had mastered several Chinese dialects. This drawing was completed in 1832.

made him an invaluable interpreter and his services were often in demand by the western merchants. When he went inland he distributed not only Bible tracts and translations of the scriptures but ointments and pills and he was said to have "a persuasive way with the inhabitants and was used to roughing it in all weathers."[4]

William Jardine is credited, however, with the most spectacular coup. He succeeded in persuading Gutzlaff to act as interpreter on one of his ships, the *Sylph,* when it went north carrying £4,000 worth of piecegoods and opium. Jardine said in his letter to Gutzlaff: "But as the expenses of the voyage cannot be defrayed from this source (the piecegoods) we have no hesitation in stating to you openly that the principal reliance is on opium. Though it is our earnest wish that you should not in any way injure the grand object you have in view by appearing interested in what by many is considered an immoral traffic, yet such traffic is so absolutely necessary to give any vessel a reasonable chance of defraying her expenses, that we trust you will have no objection to interpret on every occasion when your services may be requested."[5]

The letter ended by hinting that the more profitable the mission, the better the commission he could expect and as a further inducement a magazine which Gutzlaff was printing in Chinese was guaranteed for six months. Gutzlaff found the offer too good to refuse. He wrote in his memoirs of his three voyages around the coast of China: "After much consultation with others and a conflict in my own mind, I embarked upon the *Sylph.*" He and Mr Hugh Hamilton Lindsay, supercargo of the *Sylph* for whom the Chinnery sketch of Gutzlaff was intended, returned from this second voyage on September 5, 1832.[6]

One of Chinnery's best known and most frequently published pictures of his Macau period is that of a group of merchants relaxing on a spacious verandah overlooking the bay of Macau. It is entitled *On Dent's Verandah* (the home being that of Thomas Dent, a well-known British merchant-trader) and the three figures in the picture are the French merchant and former captain of a brig, Mr Durand, W. C. Hunter, who has been frequently quoted in the course of this book, and Captain W. H. Hall, commander of the armed East India Company ship *Nemesis,* one of the first iron-plate paddle steamers to travel round the Cape of Good Hope to China.

It is not only a striking portrait but typifies the graceful life of ease that many British and European merchants enjoyed in Macau and Canton. It recalls a remark attributed to Chinnery by Captain Arthur Cunynghame, A. D. C. to Major General Lord Saltoun, when speaking about how the East India Company employees spent their days. "Sir," said Chinnery, "they spent six months in Macau having nothing to do, and the other six months in Canton, Sir, doing nothing. Ah, Sir, those were fine days in the time of the Company."

Chinnery painted many prominent people and visitors and it is not possible to mention more than a few of the better-known personalities. After their marriage he painted Dr and Mrs Colledge, though these were separate portraits, one of Caroline Shillaber Colledge and the other of the doctor at work in his clinic. Colledge was appointed surgeon to the British Factory in 1826 and the next year began administering to the illnesses of "such indigent natives as sought his assistance." He soon found, however, that one of the most troublesome complaints for which the local Chinese medicine shops had no treatment, was diseases of the eyes.

The Chinese Repository [7] recalls that he rented apartments in Macau and that one of his patients was suffering from a massive tumour weighing, according to one report, 17 lbs. The man, Hoo Loo, was sent to England for an operation but though the tumour was removed successfully in Guy's Hospital, London, he did not survive the ordeal.

At Colledge's ophthalmic hospital, however, his success was phenomenal and in four years he treated some 6,000 cases. The Chinese Recorder and Missionary Journal states that Chinnery "obtained the consent of Mr Colledge to make an act of his practical humanity the subject of a picture, which would at once combine portrait with history."

Chinnery chose one of Colledge's cases for the theme of the painting. A 14-year-old boy had brought in an elderly Chinese woman, blind with cataract, to the hospital and Dr Colledge later operated on her successfully. The picture shows the doctor turning from his final examination of the woman's eyes, with his hand still resting on her forehead, to speak to an old servant who then translated the instructions to the patient. The 14-year-old boy is shown in the picture having prepared a chop or Chinese letter, expressing his gratitude to Dr Colledge. In the background is a man with his eyes bandaged following an operation for cataract, waiting to see the doctor.

In addition to the eye hospital, Dr Colledge also opened in 1828 the Canton Dispensary with a Dr Bradford and for a number of years they gave medical treatment to a large number of Chinese people.

For many years the portrait of Dr Colledge was missing but it has just been found again in a private collection in the United States and identified by the Chinnery expert, Mr Francis B. Lothrop of the Peabody Museum. He writes: "This is a most handsome 33 inch by 33 inch oil, regrettably in poor condition." This was the portrait mentioned in Harriet Low's diary and which she saw in London on her way home from Macau.

As for the portrait of Caroline Shillaber Colledge, Harriet's schoolmate, its whereabouts are unknown though there is a sketch in the possession of the great great grand-daughter now living on the east coast of Scotland.

Two other celebrities to be painted by Chinnery were William Jardine and James Matheson who proved to be good and loyal friends to the artist. It is clear from correspondence that Chinnery respected and admired them, though one hopes for more reasons than that they put a good deal of business his way.

The portrait of Jardine, measuring 24 inches by 19 inches, is a striking composition, apparently painted in his study in Canton for in the background is an open window, showing the foreign Factories. The portrait of Matheson is smaller, measuring 11½ inches by 9½.

The two men welcomed the arrival of a professional artist in their midst both for the landscapes and portraits he painted and for the values he represented.[8] A letter from Chinnery to Matheson shows that the relationship was much more than that of casual acquaintance: "On my coming home yesterday I selected the volume of my sketches for which you flatter me so highly by wishing to have. How grateful I am to give it to you you may suppose!"

While other merchants in Macau notably Dent, commissioned work from Chinnery, his relationship with William Jardine and James Matheson remained close. They acted as his financial advisers and, with their connections in Calcutta, helped to sort out his problems of debts. Poor Chinnery needed them. His financial worries continued unresolved for at least 16 years after his arrival in Macau. There is a surviving letter dated August 16, 1841, from Matheson "about Mr Chinnery's affairs" to his agent in Calcutta, George Gordon, re-establishing credit for 16,000 rupees "with a request that they will pay it either to any receiver regularly appointed who will grant a discharge, or to you." The letter goes on to say, "by the

104

enclosed copy of the letter of Licence, etc, granted by Chinnery's creditors . . . you will perceive he is entitled to a release provided he pays to the Trustees the moiety of his gross earnings for five years from March 11, 1836."[9]   There was some hitch, however, because Chinnery had not paid the money promptly and Matheson was asking Gordon to try and sort it out; the outcome of the case is unknown.

Matheson was not just a financial adviser but a kind friend who did his best on this occasion to shield Chinnery from the bad news of this new crisis over his debts.   Matheson wrote "the purport (being) so very unexpected and disheartening I did not venture to communicate it to him all at once."   In addition to being an honorary client of Jardine and Matheson, and a painter, Chinnery was treated with great courtesy by them and was a frequent guest at their parties.   He writes of "being up till half past one at our delightful party – but I was out at 7 and got some good drawings, but business today I fear for." [10]

Another sitter to Chinnery was Captain Robert Bennet Forbes, of the firm of Russell & Co who arrived in Macau in October, 1838, and later became Taipan though he left for New York on July 7, 1840.   Forbes wrote an amusing manuscript on the Chinnery picture which was entitled *History of a Portrait.* [11]

It begins: "In the winter of 1832 I underwent the infliction of a sitting to George Chinnery at Canton, for a half sized portrait, to be sent to my friends in the United States" – this clearly refers to Capt Forbes' earlier visit to Canton as a sea captain, before returning to become a partner of Russell & Co.

The portrait then takes up the story "I first saw the light under the hands of that Prince of Gastronomers, George Chinnery.   Whoever has not heard of that living monument of the extreme caprices of nature in making a man whose powers of stomach were equal to the ostrich, and only exceeded by his extreme ugliness, will be satisfied with a short description of his person and character.   He had been 30 years in India and deservedly obtained (according to his own account) the title of Sir T. Lawrence of the East.   He left Calcutta partly on account of pecuniary embarrassments, and partly because his wife had the double mortification of being uglier than himself and, having become aware of certain peccadillos to which he had become addicted, had made his home anything but a bower of roses, he emigrated to China.

"With nothing particularly disgusting in the appearance of his person there was an approach to the orang-outang in features and manners, mixed up with a drollery of expression, both of feature and speech, that rendered it impossible for anyone sitting to him not to smile when he opened that bottomless pit, which in the species alluded to would have been called the mouth.   He made it a rule to walk abroad every morning early to take a sketch and he required but the most distant allusion to breakfast to consider himself invited, and as it is the custom at Canton for the residents to walk before breakfast in the public square, he generally selected a victim from among those who knew best how to appreciate a solid dejeune.   He was not absolutely a bore, as he possessed great powers of conversation, and some wit, and when beginning to be satiated, he always made an effort to be grateful to his host for curry and rice received, and launched into lively conversation.

"Such was the man who (to use an expression of his own) considered 'the art of conversation as the art of painting'.   Under his auspices I found myself called into existence on a piece of canvas about 10 by 15 inches; he would take a look at me and then at my prototype, and puffing out his expansive cheeks would grunt an approval, and pointing with the handle of his brush in the most formal and pompous manner to the right or to the left, as he wished him whose form I was to bear, to turn a little one way or the other, he would say 'that's it', 'that's it' and dash away again, relating his happy experiences at the table of his last friend or, thinking of his dinner, would give an account of it in advance in such glowing terms as almost to satisfy or spoil the appetite of a moderate man like my original."

The painting was duly completed but "as my master required a copy of me for a friend in Canton, I was transferred to the shop of Lamqua, where I was hung up" and "after a few days' detention I was copied after a fashion and sent to my master."

The whereabouts of the original Chinnery painting is not known. The manuscript records that it was stolen by a starving Irish immigrant after its arrival in America but subsequently was recovered and restored to the owner. However, the painting now hanging in Captain Robert Bennet Forbes' House in Milton, Massachusetts, USA, measures 9½ by 8 inches whereas the manuscript describes the Chinnery canvas as being 10 by 15 inches. The surviving portrait could therefore be a copy, though whether Lamqua's or another artist's is uncertain.

A prominent Parsee was another of Chinnery's sitters in Macau. This was the great Bombay merchant, Sir Jamsetje Jejeebhoy, who won esteem in his own country both as a trader and particularly as benefactor of hospitals, educational and religious institutions. It was said that he gave to charity around Rs 41 lakhs. He was knighted in 1842 and made a baronet 15 years later, the first Indian to receive such an honour. [12] In his native Bombay so highly was he revered that his statue was erected. Jejeebhoy made many visits to Canton.

Several portraits of Sir Jamsetje survive in Hongkong, London, and India but how many were painted by Chinnery is uncertain. One massive canvas measuring 80 inches by 60 inches is owned by Jardine, Matheson and Co Ltd but is not the work of Chinnery. It shows Sir Jamsetje as an older man.

There was of course one other notable member of Macau society whose portrait Chinnery painted, not once but on a number of occasions. It is this sitter who will be the subject of the next chapter.

Several portraits, attributed to Chinnery and purporting to show Sir Jamsetje Jejeebhoy Bart, have come to light in recent years. The above painting is of Sir Jamsetje and his Chinese scribe.

— Courtesy Sir John Keswick, K.C.M.G.

This pagoda was sketched by Chinnery in 1831. It was situated half-way between Canton and Whampoa and in the following year he sketched this attractive landscape of Macau, and apparently squared it off later for a painting.

These two views of Canton were drawn in 1832 during one of Chinnery's visits to the city. The upper picture shows the fire appliance outside the British East India Company headquarters, while the other shows a river scene in Canton.

The sketch of the sleeping child has the following shorthand note: "Drawn and filled up pencil. August 20th, 1845".

The studies in the lower picture were apparently made in preparation for a portrait. The shorthand notes at the side say: "The left leg of the big boy crossed over the right leg would be better and the dog brought forwards so as to fill up the space it would make. Good and very useful. Aug 15th 1836."

12

'Fascinatingly ugly'

L ONG before Harriet Low described him as "fascinatingly ugly" Chinnery seems to have come to a similar conclusion himself. His "ugliness" admittedly grew more apparent with the years; this is evident from the series of self-portraits he painted, sketched or executed in chalks and ink between his middle India years and his old age in Macau.

It was not, however, a repulsive ugliness; he had a good deal of character and his garrulous, egocentric and often cheerful personality, combined to give him distinction. There was indeed an uglier man in Macau, Chinnery's journalist friend, W. W. Wood, who had been pock-marked from an early age and a contemporary recalls that Chinnery once teasingly reproached him with these words: "Oh, you wicked man! I was someone until you came. You are marked, it is true, but I was remarked. Passers-by would say 'There goes Chinnery; what an ugly fellow.' Poco, poco, my title became undisputed. What a triumph! now you would carry off the palm. Oh, you ugly piece of wood." [1]

Chinnery painted, sketched or coloured at least 14 self-portraits in a space of about 40 years and while many artists in his day painted themselves it seems that in his often lonely exile he took a special interest – indeed almost pride – in painting his own face and form.

His 1840 self-portrait which he sent to the Royal Academy in London in 1845, ranks with his portraits of the two Hong merchants, Howqua and Mowqua, as a masterpiece. It is clear from a preliminary drawing in pencil and ink, now in the Irish National Portrait Gallery, that Chinnery planned this work meticulously. He squared off the page so that he had a detailed plan in miniature for his painting and a major British collector of Chinnery's drawings has said that "it might not be easy to name a better English portrait of this period." [2]

Mr Richard Ormond, in whose office in the National Portrait Gallery in London this painting now hangs, says that it is Chinnery's most complete statement about himself and his art.[3] Indeed it deserves a permanent place on display in the Gallery.

As a composition it is beautifully balanced; it shows the artist among his favourite paintings – the familiar Mosque which he painted frequently in India, standing on the easel, and a framed picture of the stately buildings on the Praya Grande of Macau, on the wall behind.

It is an arresting painting in its composition, its colour, its technique and its detail. And of course it is the artist himself who comes out best. There he sits, straight-backed, a trifle pompous with his legs crossed and a smart dark coat, white trousers and black shoes. A white high-winged collar marks out the resolute jaw line and the protruding lower lip overhangs a bulbous chin, his long nose supporting spectacles, the intense eyes surmounted by bushy eyebrows and his head crowned with a shock of grey-white hair.

Notice the background, always interesting in any Chinnery portrait; the diagonal of the curtain is almost parallel with the easel. In the left foreground the elegant table carries two mixing bowls, sketch pad and a bottle. Below the table is a portfolio of paintings, edged in white, with hanging tapes.

It is Mr Ormond again who draws our attention to "the carefully balanced rectangles and parallelograms of the landscapes, and the struts of the easel and chair give to the composition a taut and geometrical construction. Everything is clearly defined and related." [4]

Looking at this picture one feels that Captain Robert Forbes who compared him to an orang outang, was being a trifle unfair in not also acknowledging that he had a face full of character, intelligence, humour and shrewdness.

In his self-portraits, particularly in the oils, Chinnery has done greater credit to himself than to almost any other sitter and it is possible to understand how one so engrossed in himself had little time for his wife and children. His hypochondria and his gluttony appear to be two other facets of this self-centredness which at times verges on narcissism. This trait in Chinnery seems to have developed as a result of the adulation he received following his successes in Madras, Dacca and Calcutta and it may also have been responsible for the growing impatience he showed during these years towards clients who came to his studio to be painted.

There is only one known self-portrait which falls below his usual high standard, and that is a pencil and water-colour sketch on paper formerly in the Chater Collection in Hongkong. James Orange's *The Chater Collection* [5] shows this lost self-portrait where the artist has obviously seated himself in front of a mirror. The composition is awkward and stilted and the pose unnatural and as Mr Ormond says, the bulky figure of Chinnery is almost on top of the easel, with his painting arm hidden behind the chair ending in a ridiculously small hand. [6]

Most of the self-portraits are small oils, of about nine inches by eight inches or smaller. They show Chinnery seated, half length or head and shoulders, full face, and in one owned by the Hongkong and Shanghai Bank he presents us with an interesting profile.

These paintings are scattered around the world. One, a miniature painted between 1810 and 1815 is now in the Royal Academy. Another, painted between 1835-40 is in the Peaboby Museum in Salem, Massachusetts. This was formerly owned by the Bowring family, descendants of Sir John Bowring, Governor of Hongkong from 1854 to 1859. Another painted in 1835 is owned by Sir William Keswick.

There are three known chalk and water colour self-portraits, one owned by Mr J. M. Braga and the other two by the Victoria and Albert Museum. The latter two are on either side of a piece of paper and are thought by the Museum to be studies for the painting in the National Portrait Gallery. Yet another self-portrait is in the National Gallery of Scotland [7] though for some time it was wrongly attributed to the Scottish painter, William Yellowlees. Another small oil is in the Metropolitan Museum, New York. Previously undocumented self-portraits continue to turn up and another has been reported at the Asiatic Society in Calcutta. [8]

In addition to Chinnery's large self-portrait, the National Portrait Gallery in London possesses a rough pencil sketch (4¾ by 4 ins) done in 1832 which contains shorthand notes, though these appear to refer to his landscape technique and not the self-portrait. If this was a sketch for a larger portrait its whereabouts are not known, though it is possible that it was another of Chinnery's experimental attempts to achieve a satisfactory composition.

Two small pencil sketches of himself have also been found in the Victoria and Albert Museum's massive collection of drawings bequeathed by the late James Orange. One appears to be an early self-portrait. The other is a small sketch in an oval outline which looks as if it might have been a preliminary for a miniature.

Why did Chinnery paint or draw so many pictures of himself? As has been noted it was not unusual for artists of his time to turn out a number of self-portraits but in Chinnery's case it may be assumed that living on his own and with possibly long gaps to fill in between commissions or when the weather prevented him from going out on excursions to paint landscapes or sketch, he turned to his mirror for ideas and inspiration — and found it frequently.

Chinnery eventually sent his 1840 masterpiece to the Royal Academy for exhibition. He sent it through his friend Lancelot Dent but in his letter of August 29, 1845, he made one curious stipulation — "my particular wish (is) that it should not be engraved during my lifetime — but after my Death I can have no objection."

The letter continues: "I have put within the case my written directions as to its being varnished — I now send a Certificate which will save you some trouble, I believe, at the Custom House in London."

This last paragraph recalls a letter which Chinnery many years earlier wrote to William Hickey, the diarist, who was taking home some paintings from India. As it demonstrates the care with which the artist packed his oils it is worth recording here. Chinnery wrote: "You will find the warm cloth and tin case an effectual security; the pictures are rolled on a hollow cylinder and between each is a piece of green silk to prevent their sticking to each other. You will be careful to have them gently warmed by a fire as you unroll them. In rolling them they were each made properly pliable by a regular heat."

There was a tragic postscript to this particular consignment. Hickey wrote later that while the artist had with infinite care packaged and prepared the paintings for the voyage, the Customs in London had committed a frightful atrocity in "inspecting" them.

"The tin case," wrote Hickey later, "in which he had packed them, was literally beaten to pieces, although there was a lid which could have been opened with the smallest trouble. They preferred, from sheer mischief, committing the unwarranted violence. The scoundrelly Customs Officers battered the tin to pieces and instead of taking the pictures out gradually, one by one, in the manner Chinnery had directed, they actually tore them from the rollers, without caring whether one, two or three of them were together or not, whereby everyone of them was damaged, and three completely and irreparably damaged. The most infamous part of the transaction was the presumption that the paintings were foreign — and why? Because painted out of England. There is an old Act of Parliament evidently made for the encouragement and benefit of British artists, by discouraging the import of paintings from other countries. They actually considered Chinnery a foreigner."

Clearly he took no risks with his self-portrait and declared it properly. According to Mr Richard Ormond the painting was exhibited in 1846 where it aroused little interest. One reviewer [9] "wished that the extremities had not been so neglected" while another was offended by "the annoying stab of carmine on the lower lip". The self-portrait was either given to Dent by the artist after its return from London, or was purchased following Chinnery's death. [10]

Chinnery's last known self-portrait is in the collection of Sir William Keswick, a pencil and water-colour sketch on paper, 4½ by 3½ ins. It shows the artist aged 70, nearly bald with a few whiffs of hair and a pinched expression and with fatigue showing in his face. The portrait by the French artist, G. A. Durran, now in the Peabody Museum and sketched in 1844, confirms this. In the four years since he painted his masterpiece he had aged noticeably but nevertheless he continued to sketch and paint to within a few months of his death.

V. A. M.

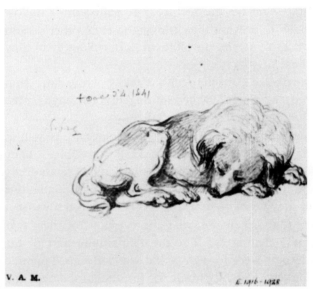

V. A. M.

Goats, pigs, cows, horses, mules, dogs, cats, chickens, and parrots were among the many animals that Chinnery sketched in India and Macau. The ink drawing of a mule and the sketch of the horses' heads above were done in Macau, the latter in 1840.

V. A. M.

13

The big exodus

IN the year 1839 the opium crisis came rapidly to a head and burst, engulfing the British community in Macau. On March 18, the formidable new Imperial Commissioner, Lin Tse-hsu, armed with full powers to eradicate the opium traffic forever, issued his edict to the British merchants.

All their opium was to be delivered to the Chinese Government and the Chinese Hongs were to report on the merchants involved and the number of chests they possessed; foreign traders had to give an undertaking that never would their vessels bring opium into China again and that if any was found doing so he could expect no mercy.

To reinforce his edict, Commissioner Lin confined all the merchants to their Factories and forbade them to leave for Macau. He also put pressure on Howqua and Mowqua to force the opium traders to give up their supplies. When the two Hong merchants returned offering 1,037 chests he is said to have turned on them angrily and asked: "Do you think my words are only air? There are tens of thousands of chests and I have demanded them all." [1]

Five days later Howqua and Mowqua reappeared at the Factories stripped of their buttons of rank and with chains round their necks like criminals being led to execution. [2] On the following Sunday the British merchants in Canton attended church twice [3] once to hear a sermon on "What is our life?" and the other "We must all appear before the judgment throne of Christ." Their prayers were answered when at 6 p.m. that night Captain Charles Elliot, the Chief Superintendent of the Trade of British Subjects in China, arrived from Macau and took charge. After a trip down the river, the last few miles of which he stood in the ship's gig wearing full uniform and outwitting pursuit and attempts by the Chinese navy to stop him, Elliot stepped ashore and ordered the flag hoisted to the British Factory masthead.

Although the Factories were well stocked with food, the faithful Hong merchants continued to smuggle in fresh supplies; the only inconvenience was that the merchants had to do their own cooking and washing up. [4] Elliot resolved, however, to deliver up the opium and guaranteed that the merchants would be indemnified later. On March 28, a total of 20,283 chests worth, at cost prices $10-11 million was made ready for delivery and on May 21 this was completed. Not satisfied with this Lin next ordered 16 of the principal opium importers to sign a promise to leave Canton forever and on Elliot's recommendation they did so. On May 24, Elliot accompanied by all British subjects left Canton for Macau. [5]

But the trade started up again east of Canton and, involving as it did Chinese smugglers, Elliot was powerless to stop it. Fears of a head-on clash between China and the opium merchants grew. In the first week of July, 1839, a drunken affray occurred near Hongkong when sailors from British and American ships, drawn to these waters by the crisis in

Canton earlier in the year, went ashore, became involved with villagers and finally killed a man.   Lin heard of the incident, determined to capitalise on his success over the opium seizures and demanded the guilty seaman be handed over to be tried by a Chinese Court.   Captain Elliot put six of the rioters on trial before a court on board ship but although one man was accused of murder the jury found there was insufficient evidence and acquitted him.   Lin ridiculed the finding and again demanded the man.   Elliot refused and Lin stopped all British trade – a formality as it turned out because it had already stopped at Canton – and next marched on Macau with a body of troops with the object of forcing the British into submission.

Their Chinese servants began to leave; the shop-keepers in Macau became very uncivil and refused to deliver food and the Portuguese "made it quite clear that they regarded their guests as tiresome encumbrances".[6]   Elliot decided it was no longer safe for British residents to remain in Macau and advised them to sail for Hongkong and take refuge there on merchant ships anchored in the harbour.   The day set for the exodus was Monday, August 26, 1839.

One batch had in fact left a few days earlier and following the piracy of a small schooner called the *Black Joke* in which the one passenger and all but one of the crew were murdered, the British were almost in a state of panic.   The night before the second group left there were fears of an armed attack on all British houses by the Chinese soldiers.   The next day, the weary, frightened British residents – men, women and children – gathered their baggage and hurried through the streets "amidst a terrible excitement of the whole population, expecting every moment a massacre by the soldiers".   They assembled on the Praya under the watchful eyes of 900 Portuguese soldiers, headed by the Governor.[7]   The British residents took off in a fleet of small boats, schooners and lorchas, and the Chinese Repository reported that it presented "an affecting spectacle as it moved slowly away from the harbour" with the Portuguese Governor,   Adriao Accacio da Silveira Pinto, seeing them off with a hollow salute.

That Chinnery was living in Macau at that time is known.   Drawings have been found dated June, 1839.   There is a good deal of uncertainty, however, over whether Chinnery left with the British community or somehow managed to stay put. Captain W. H. Hall of the paddle-steamer *Nemesis* (one of the three men Chinnery painted in the picture of *Dent's Verandah*) indicates that the British residents left in batches as Lin's anger increased.   While some went to Hongkong, others went to live on board different merchant ships.   But Captain Hall's account makes clear that the "whole British community left the place" and this suggests no exceptions.

Others believe Chinnery was ill at the time and could not move from his bed though it is unlikely that if Chinnery had been the exception and stayed in Macau this fact would have gone unrecorded.

After forcing the British out,   Commissioner Lin ordered a triumphal march through Macau and Maurice Collis writes that "soon after sunrise Lin's long procession was seen winding in, escorted by a body of Portuguese troops which had been sent to meet it."   Lin was carried in a splendid sedan by eight porters, preceded by an officer on horseback and a troop of men beating gongs and holding fluttering banners.   In the rear was the Viceroy of Kwangtung.   At the temple near the village of Mongha were displayed presents of silver, silk, tea, pigs and bullocks with their horns decorated with scarlet ribbons.   After refreshing himself with tea, Lin was carried to the city gate near the Church of St Anthony where a salute was fired from the guns of the fort.   Lin's force then made a circuit of the town, finally parading down the whole length of the Praya Grande and the Chinese inhabitants erected *pai laus* decorated with scrolls expressing their "profound gratitude for the visit of His Excellency, the

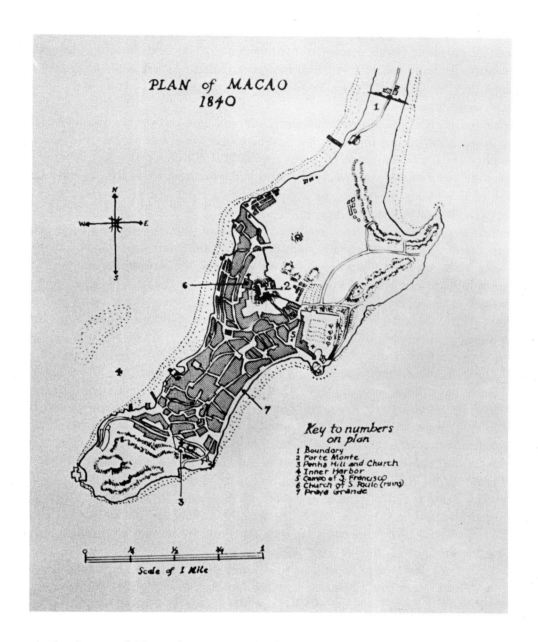

PLAN of MACAO
1840

Key to numbers
on plan
1 Boundary
2 Forte Monte
3 Penha Hill and Church
4 Inner Harbor
5 Campo of S. Francisco
6 Church of S. Paulo (ruins)
7 Praya Grande

Scale of 1 Mile

A sketch map of Macau by Warner Varnham, dated 1840. The eastern waterfront and beach known as the Praya Grande which Chinnery sketched and painted on many occasions, has been almost wholly swallowed up by reclamation. The praya is still there, lined today with graceful old banyan trees. Chinnery's residence no longer stands but the street in which it was situated, Rua Ignacio Baptista, is still there and in Varnham's map would be roughly between the points of the arrows, No. 3 and 7.

High Commissioner, who had saved them from a deadly vice and removed from them a dire calamity by the destruction of the foreign mud." [8]

If Chinnery had been in Macau it would have been a magnificent picture to paint. In the Victoria and Albert Museum collection there is an intriguing sketch of what at first sight looks like a wedding ceremony, with a team of men carrying gongs and fluttering banners, and a troop of soldiers carrying spears. As one researcher remarked there is so much action in this simple pencil sketch it looks as if they are going to walk off the page. There is another similar sketch in the same collection.

There were many Chinese troop movements at this time and processions in Macau itself would not have been an uncommon sight. Where and when did he see this scene? The usually methodical Chinnery recorded dates on his sketches but this one has none (though drawings on the same page are dated April, 1839) and we are left to wonder whether this lively sketch was of a wedding procession or a picture dating from this prolonged period of crisis in the lives of the British residents in Macau.

The British residents crossed to the more placid waters of Hongkong and spent the autumn there. They lived aboard ships in the harbour, and "on one side there was an almost barren rock, unable to supply provisions for the 2,000 British subjects now crowded together on shipboard in a starving condition, and on the other they saw a large Chinese camp in process of construction on the Kowloon peninsula, with two shore batteries on Tsimshatsui. Provisions were obtainable with great difficulty from Chinese junks and bumboats, but prices were very high." [9]

Fresh negotiations were begun with Governor Pinto to readmit the British to Macau. These failed and the refugees soon found they had jumped from the frying pan into the fire. Harassing attacks were made on the British ships and Commissioner Lin directed the magistrates of neighbouring districts to prohibit the supply of provisions to the British fleet and commanded the people to fire on British subjects whenever they went ashore. The Royal Navy succeeded in breaking this blockade and forced Lin to rescind his proclamation. Shortly after however, Lin tightened the screws again but despite this in October, 1839, the first British refugees began filtering back to Macau. [10]

There is a famous letter written by Chinnery in Macau to Matheson, which has been quoted on many occasions. In it he says: "I am at the top of my stairs, living in the greatest misery, I assure you. To be away is everything to me. I should like to paint a few good pictures before I'm put to the sword. Rely on it, something serious, if not dreadful is coming. I need not say how happy I'd be to come out if I dared. I dare not. I was out to breakfast last Sunday and was accosted coming home: 'Mr C. you are a bold man to be walking about!'... I passed a night of horror and presentiment not to be told. I ran down to the doctor the other night in fear and trembling. I do not go out again, I think, until I cross the beach."

Most authorities who have quoted this letter have assumed it was written prior to or during the crisis of August, 1839, but the date on the letter shows it to have been written on February 23, 1840, almost six months after the British exodus. This indicates that if Chinnery did in fact leave with the others he had slipped back into Macau.

By this time, tension was still running high between Commissioner Lin and the British. The first battle of Chuenpi had taken place in the Pearl River estuary and following it a protracted cannonade from Tsimshatsui had forced the British merchantmen in Hongkong harbour to leave for Tungku, 12 miles to the west. [11] The Portuguese Governor of Macau had refused to permit the storing of British cargoes in the warehouses of that city and to make matters worse, posters were put up on the walls of Macau inciting the Chinese to murder all British residents.[12]

It was because of this that on February 4 a British man-of-war, the *Hyacinth*, under the command of Captain Smith sailed into the inner harbour to evacuate British residents. This caused alarm, indignation and consternation. Governor Pinto and the Senate declared their neutrality violated and ordered Captain Smith to sail out again.[13] He did so, leaving the British in Macau to an uncertain fate. The tension continued for at least the next three weeks.

Whether there were further attempts at evacuation is not known, but Chinnery's letter written 19 days later contains an intriguing sentence — "I do not go out again, I think, until I cross the beach." — which prompts one to ask whether he was speaking metaphorically or literally. If the latter, it will be recalled from Chinnery's own painting of the Praya Grande that for anyone to embark on a ship in the harbour it was necessary to catch a sampan from the beach below the praya or sea wall. Chinnery's oil in the City Museum and Art Gallery in Hongkong and his brilliant water colour in the National Gallery of Ireland show this beach clearly, with the sampans standing off shore, and it is also indicated in Warner Varnham's map of Macau of 1840. Could it have been that the British were considering another exodus? Once again we are left to guess and perhaps the only way we shall be able to determine Chinnery's activities and movements at this time and afterwards is by a detailed study of his drawings, which in most cases carry a date and sometimes notes.

By July of that year, however, British residents, whether living on board ships or in Macau, were able to breathe more easily as the build-up of British naval and military forces gathered pace. This included three line-of-battle ships mounting 74 guns each, 13 other ships of war, a troopship and four armed steamers from the East India Company fleet as well as 27 transports with three regiments aboard, a large number of volunteers from Bengal and a corps of Madras sappers.

Chinnery noted the arrival of the first armed East India Company steamer, the *Madagascar* under Captain Dicey. A shorthand note has been found on a sketch which says: "Arrival of the first steamer. The greatest day for the English in China." It proved to be a prophetic statement. The steamers played an invaluable role in the forthcoming naval engagements by towing the British fleet into position for bombardments, landing troops at vital positions and negotiating shallow portions of the river where a sailing ship might easily become marooned on a sandbank.[14]

The Lin demarche and the unfriendly and unco-operative attitude of the Portuguese Governor, however, delivered a blow to Macau from which it never recovered.

Although a number of British families returned rather than endure the hell of shipboard life it was apparent to most that they needed a more secure base than Macau, with its vacillating and unpredictable Governor. From 1840 it was Hongkong that the British increasingly looked upon as their centre of operations, if not yet their home. Chinnery was one of the exceptions in deciding to continue living in Macau after the crisis. He had taken residence in Rua Ignacio Baptista several years earlier and it was that house he was to occupy until his death in 1852.

In 1840 Chinnery was 66 years old and in his self-portrait painted at about that time, he showed himself to be still a vigorous and robust figure. If the departure of the British residents resulted in a sharp retraction of his social outings, there were frequent visits from old friends and tourists passing through. An author of this period advised his readers when in Macau:

Two views of the Praya Grande by Chinnery.

"Be sure that you call on Chinnery, the painter; he has years on his brow, but his hand is very talented." [15]

Even before the 1839 crisis Chinnery had entertained a number of visitors to his studio. A young French artist, Auguste Borget, arrived in China in 1838 after a sketching tour of the United States and South America. He later published a book of sketches of China and the Chinese. A friend of Honore de Balzac, Borget had a style of painting not unlike Chinnery's. His water-colours of Hongkong and Canton show him to be one of the more talented artists to visit the Far East. For many years scholars speculated whether he and Chinnery ever met during his 10-month stay, and indeed in the Catalogue to the exhibition of the Peabody Museum in 1967 the Hon. Trustee, Mr Francis Lothrop had written: "It seems almost impossible that he did not meet Chinnery." A subsequent letter from Mr Lothrop announced that the evidence of the meeting had at last turned up — and in a most unexpected way.

The family of a well-known American tea merchant in Canton, Gideon Nye Jnr, who went bankrupt, discovered some of his old papers and turned them over to the Old Dartmouth Society which is the historical society of New Bedford, Massachusetts. The director, Mr Richard Kugler, recognised Chinnery's name on a torn piece of paper and it turned out to be a mutilated copy of the Nye bankruptcy sale and listed some of the pictures sold. One was described as "scene near Macao: by M. Borget — as an interchanged gift to Mr Chinnery".

This same document showed that Chinnery had met another visiting French artist in 1834. This was Admiral Paris of the French Navy, who at that time was a young lieutenant and who later became a famous author and artist on Pacific native craft and head of the Marine section of the Louvre in Paris. The young lieutenant had given Chinnery a picture of the Temple at Mongha, which five years later was to be the scene of a display of presents for Commissioner Lin as he made his triumphal procession around Macau. [16]

Even after the exodus and the establishment of Hongkong, Chinnery continued to receive visitors and Captain Arthur Cunynghame, ADC to Major General Lord Saltoun reported after meeting the old artist that "he spoke with fondness of the old days in the Company's time as being the pleasantest recollections of his life, detailing with great fervour the splendid life they lived in Canton, being evidently no mean gastronomist himself."

Cunynghame wrote that "although his powerful genius meets with the best reward it can do there, yet the field is small and contracted . . . well was I rewarded when I paid him my accustomed visit, not only enjoying the repast of criticising his countless productions of art, but listening to those numberless anecdotes which he had invariably at command, and which he told with such spirit and naivete."

There has been much speculation about Chinnery's income and financial position during these days when there was a dwindling business for oil paintings and when the Chinese painter Lamqua was providing strong competition. Certainly it seems that he lived modestly and I am indebted to two researchers in Macau for their discoveries in the city archives that Chinnery had a bad record for non-payment of rent. Mr Luis Gomes has found an order in the records of the Municipal Council requiring Chinnery to pay his landlord back rent for the year October 1, 1836-37, while Fr Manuel Teixeira has found that from 1846 to the year of his death he in fact paid no rent for his lodgings at 8 Rua Ignacio Baptista.

He continued to sketch, however, and made up small albums which he sold. There is a surviving letter to Mr R. J. Gilman in Hongkong in 1848 which shows that he charged 100 Spanish dollars for the book of drawings and 50 dollars for a picture (This letter is reproduced in the appendix to this book).   It would seem he produced a number of copies of these albums which he sold.   His sketches show that he continued drawing almost until his last days and he apparently managed a comfortable even if modest existence.   However Mr Francis Lothrop, who has made a careful study of Chinnery's work, has written in a letter "there is no doubt in my mind that Chinnery's work from 1846 after his visit to Hongkong until his death, shows a marked deterioration.   This is quite apparent in his sketches, charmingly drawn and definitely lacking the vigour of his earlier work.   His health may have been the cause."

Chinnery, in addition to sketching and painting also gave lessons, though the impression that some writers have given of a flourishing school for native artists is erroneous.   Besides Harriet Low and Mrs Gilman, four other pupils were the tea inspector in Canton, Warner Varnham, Robert Ellice, Dr John Scarth and Dr T. Boswell Watson.   Dr Watson attended to Chinnery throughout his final illness.[17]   One only has to read Chinnery's correspondence with his pupil in Calcutta, Mrs Browne, to realise he could never have run a school for people with whom he could not effectively communicate.   Indeed Chinnery seems to have kept his distance from Lamqua and was contemptuous of the rest of the local painters.   Not only did he not acknowledge their talents, such as they were, but it is doubtful if he mixed in Chinese circles at all except with the pidgin English-speaking Hong merchants.   His knowledge of the Chinese language was at best limited.   He also appears to have been rather scornful of Chinese art and apparently had no contact with any of the leading Chinese classical painters.[18]

In a letter written in his 74th year he confessed: "I am not without some hope that I may yet be where Art is known, felt and appreciated."   He said in another letter: "In China, art may be said to be a dead letter."   Chinnery obviously knew little of China beyond his own limited horizons though it is impossible to believe that in his 27 years in Macau he had not gained some insight into Chinese art.   Not far from Macau was a Chinese artist, Su Liu-peng, and it has been suggested that Su and Chinnery "would undoubtedly have found each other's work completely delightful even if they had absolutely nothing else in common."[19]

This is however debatable.   Chinnery was not himself influenced by Chinese traditional art which is surprising in view of the long history of chinoiserie in Europe.   Van Gogh copied Japanese woodblock prints but Chinnery did not appear to be attracted by Chinese scroll painting though he must have seen many in Canton.   For one so dedicated to art this is a strange gap in his otherwise keen interest in local customs and traditions.[20]

However, Chinnery was well known and, judging by the way he was copied, highly esteemed by local people with a knowledge of art.   His Chinese name was not very flattering – Chin Lup Lei (meaning "money to pay interest", adroitly chosen for one who often seemed to be in financial straits) – but when the time came to name a street after him on the occasion of the bicentenary of his birth in 1974, an *amende honorable* was made when the Macau authorities gave him a new name of Chin Lin Lei, meaning " 1,000 years of benefit." [21]

Whether it was the decline in business or curiosity about the newly founded colony or an invitation from an old friend we do not know, but in 1846 Chinnery took a boat across the Pearl River estuary and visited Hongkong.   This forms the subject of the next chapter.

Street scene in Macau

— Courtesy Hongkong and Shanghai Banking Corpn

Street scene in Macau

— Courtesy Hongkong and Shanghai Banking Corpn

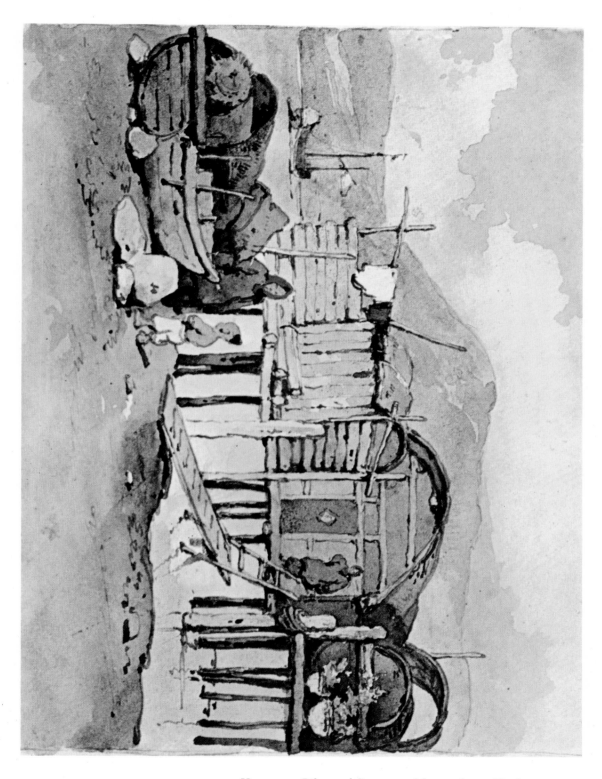

Houses on Piles and Sampans, Macau, Inner Harbor

— Courtesy Peabody Museum, Salem, Massachusetts.

Ma Chi Ping

— Courtesy Hongkong and Shanghai Banking Corpn

Self-portrait

14

'His works of art will outlive us all'

CHINNERY spent the hot, humid summer months of 1846 in Hongkong and he tells us in a surviving letter that he completed about 15 views of the new colony. The majority of these are pencil sketches though there are water colours of East Point, Jardine's original headquarters, and an oil of Victoria Peak, now owned by the Hongkong and Shanghai Bank.

Clearly the trip was a trial for the septuagenarian and he wrote that "all the time (I was there I was) so very unwell, not to say ill, that I had the power of doing but very little; and those views I made there I have commissions to execute pictures from for particular parties."

A number of these paintings and sketches survive today in London, Salem, Hongkong and Tokyo, and some are reproduced in this volume. These show the development of buildings along the foreshore of the new township. Others show Jardine, Matheson's building at East Point, with views from the east and west and a most charming picture is the water colour now in Matheson's London office showing villagers, goats, "swayback" pigs, hawkers with carrying poles and baskets, junks and lorchas in the bay and the craggy, barren Victoria Peak in the background. This is now somewhat faded but otherwise in good condition.

He also drew pictures of the main street of the young colony, named then as now, Queen's Road. This shows workmen wielding pickaxes, gamblers on the pavement, Chinese and foreign residents walking and a horseman galloping by. Another is described as Pedder's Hill, with the Harbour Master's Office, a pleasant single story bungalow, on the knoll of a hill with its tall flagstaff. Junks sail in the placid harbour waters, against the serene backdrop of the Kowloon hills.

There is another showing Murray Barracks with what is thought to be the original matshed church built on the site of what is now the Hilton Hotel. Certainly it has a bell at its eastern end suggesting if not a place of worship, a mess of some sort.[1]

He also painted a water colour of the same scene, as well as other views of Hongkong, and these are now in the Peabody Museum in Salem, Massachusetts. They are all charming pictures, sketched and painted in the artist's 72nd year and while in some cases they lack the quality of some of his earlier works they are of particular importance as early records of Hongkong, and ably complement those pictures painted by Murdoch Bruce, Auguste Borget, Marciano Baptista and others.

If it was Chinnery's intention to assess business prospects in the newly founded Colony he soon discovered that Hongkong was not without talented artists. Gradually the native artists of Macau and Canton moved into Hongkong, setting up studios in Queen's Road and, as

The frontispiece for Chinnery's sketches of Hongkong, made during his visit in 1846 (above) with a view looking west along the shoreline of Hongkong.

photography came in, they branched into new ways of making up portraits — by enlarging photographs and painting over them.

It must have been somewhat mortifying to Chinnery, however, to discover his old competitor, Lamqua, had moved in before him. A newly discovered advertisement in the Hongkong Register[2] shows that Lamqua set up business on September 1, 1845 and on a number of occasions during Chinnery's stay Lamqua's notice appeared on the front page of the Register.

It read: "Lamqua, Protrait-painter (sic), having removed his Macau establishment to Hongkong is prosecuting his profession at No 3 Oswald's Building, Queen's Road, and trusts by diligence and care to merit a continuance of the patronage with which the public have so long honoured him." Marciano Baptista was another Macau artist to move to Hongkong and he also lived in Oswald's Building though this was some years later.

Whether Lamqua's presence made any difference to the number of commissions Chinnery obtained we do not know, although for at least the next two years Chinnery was still receiving orders for copies of the drawings he made while in Hongkong. It is evident that many residents still held his work in great respect even if at this stage few were interested in having their portraits painted.

Whether it was ill-health that persuaded Chinnery to return to the peace and quiet of Macau or whether he found this new, raucous Hongkong with its mosquitoes, noise and bustle disturbing we do not know. He returned at the end of the summer and settled down to a quiet yet still active life of sketching. There are stories that as he grew older he became positively obese and could no longer walk around the town but had to be carried in a sedan chair. An old resident wrote to the South China Morning Post many years ago that "when a suitable spot offered he would tell the bearers to set him down. Sitting there he would sketch until evening, with children clustering around him, a pleasant picture of the artist's declining years." Judging from his sketching at this time he had lost none of his desire to get about. It is indeed one of the endearing features of Chinnery that even at the age of 77 or 78 he had never retired or put his work aside.

Towards the end of his life he wrote a letter which was published in the Friend of China and Hongkong Gazette on June 2, 1852, shortly after his death. In it he said: "You are very kind indeed to take part with me in my sad illness. I am not worse than I was, but very little better; the confusion and swimming in my head I the most complain of — my sight is somewhat better — I had my palette set this morning, but I could not use it! However, I by no means despair — I am certain (I think) that, with a change of weather, I shall get myself (well), as much as a man can be at near 80! Ah, how much and how continually do I think on what your kind and good note speaks of. How do I trust in that power which guides, rules and preserves us all! What can support us under our great trials but this? What my sufferings have been these three months (my only source of daily bread being prevented me) Providence only knows! But I hold up in mind — if I get well I will fear nothing — there is enough to do, and more than enough, if my physical powers are restored to me. Please God all will come right! My it be so!"

Writing of his final illness, W. C. Hunter[3] said that it was "too evident that his days were drawing to a close. Patrick Stewart, for many years a resident of Macau, to which place he had come more than 20 years before from Bombay, and Hurjeebhoy Rustonjee, a Parsee, who had passed a long time in Canton, both being old friends, and myself remained with him the last night of his life. He died at half-past four a.m. on May 30, 1852.

"After seeing his effects placed in his studio we sealed the doors, left his servant Augustine and several Chinese in charge, and I came home to bed at 5 o'clock.   An autopsy was made by Doctor Watson, our Macau medico, who attended Chinnery in his last illness, the morning of his death, about 10 o'clock, at which Stewart and myself were present.

"On examining the brain it was evident that he had died of serious apoplexy, while the stomach was wonderfully healthy – though everyone supposed from his wonderful eating powers that his stomach would be found in a most deranged disorder."

The news of his death spread quickly to Macau, Canton and Hongkong.   The obituaries appeared in the next issues of the Hongkong newspapers though in the case of the Hongkong Register the writer could not remember when he arrived in Macau.   He made a guess and said 1813.   He was out by 12 years.   He was a little more knowing about his style and accomplishments, however.   Chinnery, said the obituary, was an artist of no common merit and in his younger days executed portraits in a style hardly second to that of Sir Thomas Lawrence, while his sketches of Chinese scenery had always been highly valued for their fidelity and clearness.

The newspaper went on: "As a companion he was remarkable for the mass of anecdotes and *jeu d'esprit* which he introduced into his conversation, and few were the individuals who visited China who omitted to visit his studio."

The Overland Friend of China on June 22 said in its obituary that "For some time past his friends have seen that he was fast wearing away, and measures were in progress at the time of his decease for providing him with several additional comforts – indeed of relieving him from that anxiety as to the means of living which, to one in his feeble condition, must have been particularly trying.

"Mr Chinnery was never a provident or he would have died a rich man."

Mr Gideon Nye, an old friend of Chinnery's who came to Canton in 1833, wrote in his book of reminiscences:[4] "His ample fund of anecdote will soon be utterly forgotten but his works of Art – being the emanations of real genius, will outlive us all . . . Chinnery also had some of the so-called characteristic weaknesses of genius, with his geniality of disposition; and such an exuberance of imagination and fancy that there was gusto in much that he did approaching the grotesque.   He wielded a vigorous and facile though somewhat wayward pencil – it was Nature's self in conveying action."

A few weeks later the Register republished the obituary from the Bengal Hurkaru and it seems the Editor of that newspaper knew Chinnery a little better.   He commented that "he resembled Coleridge not only in idleness and procrastination but in his preference of conversation to work.   He was a capital punster and his remarks on men and manners were singularly shrewd, piquant and original.   His talk was always fresh.   It never wanted the characteristic fervour and enthusiasm of genius.   Though he did not turn his art to so much pecuniary profit as was within his power he loved and reverenced it on its own account.

"When the more mighty merchants of Calcutta were falling around him into ruin and contempt, he used to speak with exultation of a gift which was independent of the caprice of fortune.   'What will these poor devils do now?' he would ask.   'Some of these men who by sheer good luck came into the command of crores upon crores of rupees will now hardly earn by personal exertion an income sufficient for a cranny.   But I can never be wholly destitute.   My beautiful art will always secure me a livelihood and a name."

W. C. Hunter takes up the story again: "A few days after his death Dr Watson and I were requested by Judge Cavalho, chief judicial officer of Macau, to look through his books, papers,

136

trunks, &c, in case a will might have been left, but there was nothing of the kind. Several camphor wood trunks, however, were found, filled with pen-and-ink sketches and very choice oil paintings. At length there being no claimant for his effects, they were sold by order of the judge."

In the issue of the Hongkong Register of July 13, a notice appeared stating that his paintings and sketches would be sold by public auction on Wednesday, July 28, and following days. The day before the sale, the Hongkong Register reported that "a Regatta, a Ball, and the Works of the late Mr Chinnery at Macau have taken away the elite of Hongkong society for the present week. The people who remain wander about in disconsolate dullness, ashamed to shew themselves, as not to be at Macau argues them unknown."

How many of Chinnery's paintings and sketches were sold at auction and the prices they fetched are not, alas, recorded. It would have been interesting to compare the prices of 1852 with those of the present day. Chinnery's executors were Dent & Company, who were said to have taken over many boxes of his drawings and sold them in the following year. The partners of Jardine, Matheson were also buyers and many others of his paintings and sketches came into the possession of Wyndham O. Law, a former member of the Chinese Maritime Customs.

The last reference in the Hongkong Register of 1852 was a notice signed by Mr F. A. Da Silveira to the effect that all parties having claims against Chinnery's estate should send them in within 30 days "otherwise they will not be included in the scheme of division". We do not know how many claims were sent in, though from Fr Teixeira's research we know that his outstanding rent payments were recovered by the landlords, the Catholic Mission of Peking, from his estate. It would be interesting to know whether any claims came from Indian moneylenders in Calcutta or whether the claim mentioned by James Matheson in his letter to George Gordon in 1841 was finally settled from the estate.

Chinnery was buried in the Old Protestant Cemetery in Macau surrounded by the graves of many of his old friends and acquaintances. Gideon Nye[5] tells us that "a fund was raised for a memorial tablet to his memory; but it has not yet been received from England." This was some 21 years after Chinnery's death. A tablet was finally placed on the bare granite face of the tomb in May, 1974 when the Macau Government celebrated the bicentenary of Chinnery's birth though the day chosen was actually the 122nd anniversary of his death.

The memorial said in Chinese, Portuguese and English: "To the memory of George Chinnery, a son of William and Elizabeth Chinnery, born 5th January, 1774, at 4 Gough Sq., Fleet Street, London died 30th May at 8 Rua de Ignacio Baptista, Macao. I go on my way in the strength of the Lord."

An American critic[6] tells us that for a long time after his death Chinnery suffered from the neglect of art historians and from the attentions of the compilers of biographical dictionaries "who, gathering bits of hearsay here and there, pieced together a biography that was largely error. Although Chinnery's name and fame survived steadily in Philadelphia and Salem, in Canton and Macau and probably in Calcutta, among East Indian and China trade families it apparently made little impression on art circles in London."

Even in Hongkong Chinnery's pictures dwindled in number and when a group of local worthies decided to hold an exhibition in the City Hall in 1876 they had to confess failure for "it became evident that his works had in most cases been withdrawn from the Colony. Most possessors of them have during the 25 years that have elapsed since his death returned to their native lands and carried with them such records of his genius as they have been enabled to acquire.   The few that remain, however, have been generally forthcoming and abundantly testify to the talent of the man".[7]

As the years rolled by Chinnery became a legendary figure among the Chinese[8] and a tradition grew up that he was put to death in Peking at the ripe old age of 100 on the orders of the Emperor for molesting his favourite concubine.   In retrospect it sounds like a tall story of Chinnery's own telling but it was the beginning of the Chinnery legend which art historians from many parts of the world have embellished.   It was thanks to the thoroughness of men like W. H. Welply, J. J. Cotton, Sir William Foster and E. W. Bovill that the distortions were ironed out and in more recent times a new generation of Chinnery scholars have taken over the task of setting the record straight.   It is thanks to their efforts that this book has been possible.

A market gardener waters his vegetables in this ink drawing.

– Courtesy Victoria and Albert Museum

138

Chinnery visited Hongkong in the summer of 1846 and these sketches were undertaken at
that time. The picture above shows a building identified as the first matshed church to be
erected in the colony on the site of the present Hilton Hotel. In the background are two
buildings which have survived to the present-day, Murray Barracks and Headquarters
House; the latter is now known as Flagstaff House, the residence of the Commander British
Forces, Hongkong. The picture below is believed to be part of Queen's Road, still one of the
principal thoroughfares on Hongkong island.

Two more sketches showing views of Hongkong drawn by Chinnery in 1846. Above is the Harbour Master's Office on Pedder Hill on Hongkong island overlooking the harbour and the serene backdrop of the Kowloon hills. The picture below shows Jardine, Matheson's offices and godowns at East Point in the region occupied today by the Excelsior Hotel and the World Trade Centre.

— Courtesy Morrison Collection, Toyo Bunko, Japan.

These two water colours were painted by Chinnery for Jardine, Matheson and Co Ltd and show (above) Jardine's offices and godowns at East Point in Hongkong in 1846, and the Praya Grande, Macau.

Hongkong, about 1846. This drawing by George Chinnery was presented to the Hongkong and Shanghai Bank by Mr. A. E. Balloch of Greenwich, Connecticut, U.S.A. in 1970. It was formerly the property of his father, Mr. Gideon Balloch, who was chairman of the Hongkong and Shanghai Bank in 1910.

This landscape in oils shows the Hongkong waterfront and was painted by Chinnery during his visit in 1846.

Two sketches by Chinnery, the upper one apparently an outline in preparation for a painting. It is unfortunately undated and the figures cannot be identified. The lower picture is notable mainly for the miniature self-portrait with Chinnery's own signature underneath.

— Courtesy Victoria and Albert Museum.

Chinnery's grave in the Old Protestant Cemetery in Macau was given a commemorative plaque on the occasion of the artist's 200th anniversary in 1974. This photograph by the author shows the granite tomb with a memorial wreath placed there by the Governor of Macau, General Nobre de Carvalho.

Epilogue

AN intriguing question mark overshadows George Chinnery's life in India and Macau. What kind of an artist would he have become had he not moved to Ireland at the age of 21 after his early success in London? What would have happened had he not made a disastrous marriage which encouraged him to go to India and later Macau? Would he have joined the ranks of painters of the calibre of Turner and Constable or would he always have remained a promising painter of the second rank?[1]

Quite a few critics believe Chinnery might have become one of the great masters of the day but there are others who reject this view and one scholar[2] is convinced that "he would have always been temperamentally antipathetical to the establishment. I am sure he would have always played his cards wrong."

Chinnery remains a controversial painter to this day and there are always likely to be marked divisions of opinion on his stature and ability. What can be said is that if Chinnery had stayed in England, we would have been the poorer both in terms of scenes and pictures of the era in which he lived and of artistic influence on contemporary painters and sketchers in India and China.

For Chinnery opened many windows on life in the literally thousands of portraits, landscapes, sketches and drawings of Madras, Calcutta, Dacca, Macau, Canton, Hongkong and the Pearl River estuary. That alone is a priceless legacy.

It has been said[3] that Chinnery was an interesting painter in his own right. While his English and Irish pictures reflected the current styles of the period, those in Macau and Canton developed along an individual line, partly due to his isolation, and they had a distinct character and charm of their own. This justifiably places him among the ranks of noteworthy painters of his day and it is fair to say that even if he played no part in the development of European or British art he had some influence on Chinese artists who adopted western styles.

Between Spoilum and Lamqua, the two Chinese painters found at either end of his life span in Macau, there is a world of difference. Lamqua clearly learnt something from Chinnery and he and his contemporaries imitated his pictures closely and well enough to provide serious competition for the available business. Indeed from Lamqua to the present day one can trace the direct line of descent in the contemporary "Hongkong school" of painters, though the majority have outgrown his influence and are today pursuing independent art forms.

In the 200 years since Chinnery was born, art, its influence and appreciation have become a universal thing. Chinnery's art touched three or four relatively small parts of the world but in each he left an enduring picture of his times and in doing so planted an influence that has flourished with the years and which in turn has enriched the local culture.

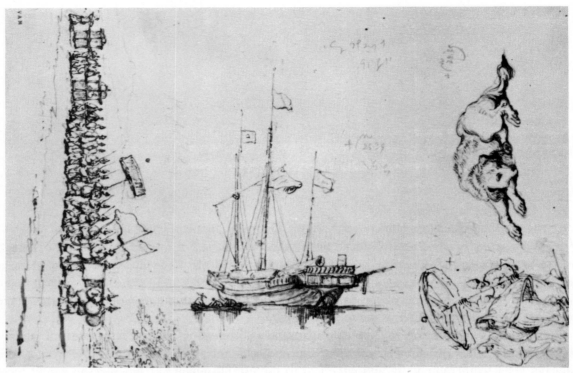

The above sketch is noteworthy for two reasons: Chinnery often filled his paper with several random sketches, some in great detail, others fairly rough. The other feature is the procession which could have been a wedding or a visit by a Chinese official. The shorthand refers to the junk. It says: "All the action excellent. The mast ought to be quite straight. April 26th, '39 ½ distance."

The lower sketch shows a ship on its side apparently off Macau. The shorthand reads: "With figures at the top of the boat. Figure coming down from the bow by the rope to re-collect. December 6th '33. Better than nothing was all that can be said for it."

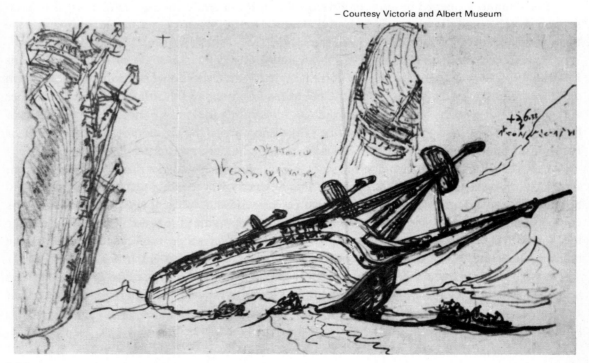

George Chinnery's Shorthand*

by

Geoffrey W. Bonsall

O NE of the characteristic features of George Chinnery's sketches which was not adequately studied until recently is his use of shorthand, not only to give a precise date to nearly all of his drawings but also, in many cases, to add annotations concerning details, colours, and draughtsmanship and sometimes, in spare spaces, to make comments not in any way related to the sketch.

It has become increasingly apparent to Chinnery scholars that, in addition to the authentication and comparative study of his oil paintings and watercolours, an understanding of his shorthand notes was important for a better appreciation of his sketches and, possibly, for rewarding insights into his life and work. With this aim in view a card catalogue has already been compiled of translations of about one thousand words, all taken from Chinnery's own shorthand writing on his drawings which are now scattered around the world.

Unlike Harriet Low, Chinnery was not a methodical diarist[1] and, as far as we know, did not make any detailed biographical record, though there is one known shorthand example of a few very brief notes for some consecutive days.[2] But, nevertheless, the dates and other translations from the shorthand on his sketches may enable us to know more about his drawing and painting techniques, to reconstruct periods in his life, and even to follow how he spent parts of certain days.

This is made possible by the fact that Chinnery dated nearly all of his drawings, as well as using a small cross near to each separate sketch. This cross is not a signature but probably means 'correct' or 'sketched' and is followed very often by the month in shorthand and then the day and year in arabic numerals. When these quick sketches were worked over or 'filled up with pen' as he put it, the same or a new date was added. This was sometimes months or even many years later. This filling up or completion was also identified by a small circle with a dot inside. Thus, once the amateur has learnt the shorthand signs for the months it is possible to date the sketches, rather like the dating of Chinese porcelain from the few characters used for the reign periods, except that there are no fakes among Chinnery sketches. Quite often the place – Canton, Macau, Hongkong, Madras, etc. is also given in shorthand.

In addition to making translations of all the available shorthand, I am also assembling a microfilm and photographic record of the sketches with copies arranged, firstly, by date so as to compile a biographic record and, perhaps, to show some of Chinnery's stylistic development and, secondly, by subject so as to indicate how the sketches were used as studies and as the basis for later watercolours and oils, for one of the common notes in his shorthand on a sketch is 'Picture at any time'. Some of his sketchbooks may also have been intended as samples both for pupils to copy and for prospective customers to choose from.[3]

The chronological and stylistic analysis is a big task because Chinnery's sketches are both numerous and widely scattered; sketches of the same subject and even those drawn on the same day have now become very distantly separated in quite different collections and parts of the world. In fact it may be worth noting here that, although Chinnery has not yet been ranked among the best artists of his time, his work has probably reached more countries than that of many of his better-known contemporaries. Fortunately some of the large collections which have facilitated the study of the shorthand are available in, for instance, the Hongkong and Shanghai Banking Corporation in Hongkong,[4] the Toyo Bunko (Oriental Library) in Tokyo,[5] the Peabody Museum in Salem, Massachusetts,[6] the Victoria and Albert Museum and the British Museum in London[7] and, in Lisbon, the Bibliotheca da Sociedade de Geographia.[8] However, many drawings owned by individuals have yet to be analysed. In a few instances the shorthand has been erased[9] or cut off, but Chinnery was a very prolific draughtsman and there are probably several thousand sketches still surviving. In the Europe of his day the ability to draw was regarded as a necessary accomplishment for the educated person, but Chinnery's unending sketching was obviously for him an essential part of his art. However, Chinnery's erratic career, the scattering of his work abroad, and his previously mysterious shorthand have all tended to hinder a true understanding of his mastery as a draughtsman and the content of his shorthand writing. The research on his shorthand is now helping to correct this situation and, in the U.S.A., Mrs Moyra Baker, formerly of the Peabody Museum has contributed with studies of his shorthand in that collection[10] and, in England, Mr Frank Higenbottam, formerly of the Royal Museum and Public Library, Canterbury has deciphered several interesting examples of Chinnery's shorthand.[11]

The existence of the shorthand on so many of Chinnery's sketches is, apart from their easily recognisable style, one almost incontrovertible way of identifying them as his. In contrast, his Chinese contemporaries such as Lamqua used no such characteristic symbols, and their copying of Chinnery's work was limited to his paintings, for they never seemed to have understood the need or use of sketches. Nor did any of his other probable or possible pupils, D'Oyly, Mrs Browne, Ellice, Varnham, Watson, Baptista, make any known use of shorthand. So it remains as Chinnery's own unwitting 'signature' – the Gurney shorthand.

It has been known for many years that the shorthand system which Chinnery used was that invented by Thomas Gurney and first published in 1750 and said to have been a development of the Mason system.[12] Other well-known early British systems of that and earlier periods were Rich's, Weston's, Shelton's, Lyle's, Mavor's and Taylor's.[13] Chinnery did in fact use almost the standard Gurney system with very few personal variations.[14] The capital letters which occur among his writings are rather his own abbreviations of words in longhand than in any way variations of the shorthand system among which they occur.

Quite apart from Chinnery's use of it, the Gurney system has a very interesting history of its own. It was widely used for about one hundred and fifty years and the handbook for the method went through at least eighteen editions[15] and was variously entitled. The eighteenth edition is simply *A text-book of the Gurney system of shorthand*, but the sixth edition of 1767 was more luxuriously called *Brachygraphy: or short-writing, made easy to the meanest capacity – The persons, moods, and tenses, being comprised in such a manner, that little more than the knowledge of the alphabet is required, to the writing hundreds* [sic] *of sentences in less time than spoken. The whole is founded on so just a plan, that it is wrote with greater expedition than any yet invented and likewise may be read with the greatest ease. Improved after upwards of thirty years practice and experience.* The handbooks are preserved in several libraries, notably the British Museum and the extensive Carlton Collection of shorthand material now in the University of London Library and gathered by the late Mr W. J. Carlton.[16] There is also a history and a little-known dictionary of the system. At least one eighteenth-century diary written in Gurney shorthand still exists.

It is not generally known that the inventor of the system, Mr Thomas Gurney, was the official shorthand writer of the Criminal Court at the Old Bailey and that Mr William Brodie Gurney was appointed in 1813 as the first shorthand writer to both Houses of Parliament. [17] Equally interesting and overlooked is the fact that the firm of W. B. Gurney and Sons, London still exists and are still verbatim reporters to Parliament, though Pitman rather than the Gurney system is now used. But the Gurney system was still being used alongside Pitman (from 1881) until well into the twentieth century, and it has been said that it would have survived even longer if it had been given the same publicity and promotion which its main rival, the new Pitman system, enjoyed. Even so there is at least one member of the firm of W. B. Gurney and Sons who studied the method, and another member of the same firm who had been a verbatim writer of the system was still alive in the 1960s.[18]

It is of particular interest to note that the novelist Charles Dickens was one of the fastest, most accurate and most famous writers of Gurney shorthand when he was a journalist and reporter as a young man. Only a few examples of his shorthand seem to have survived but other records do exist in the Gurney system and several legal documents, such as the trial of Warren Hastings in 1789 were preserved in it by Joseph Gurney.[19]

Of more special concern to Chinnery studies is the 1767 sixth edition of the Gurney handbook which includes, as one of the examples for students to copy, a page in Gurney shorthand of *Revelations*, Chapter V in the hand of William Chinnery, who must have been George Chinnery's grandfather.[20]

The connection of George Chinnery with the Gurney system thus becomes clearer and closer, and the fact that there are examples of his use of it on drawings made before he left England in 1802[21] proves that he must have learnt or been taught it as a young man, perhaps by his father or grandfather.[22] It had become a well-proved system and, before the days of female secretaries, typewriters, and recording machines, it is not at all surprising that it was widely employed by men in journalism, the legal profession and in government and perhaps business circles. Charles Dickens has left us an interesting description of his struggles to learn the system, both in *David Copperfield*, which is partly autobiographical, and in a talk which he gave in May 1865, to the second annual dinner of the Newspaper Press Fund which was also printed, in Pitman shorthand, in The Reporters' Journal.[23]

The Gurney system, like any other, requires study and practice, and it went through some variations such as in the use of shortened forms but, basically, it was and remained very simple. The handbook gives all the description for its use, the alphabet and basic rules in only about ten pages, and the attainment of reading and minimum writing ability (though not verbatim) is encouragingly fast. It is doubtful whether Chinnery was ever a verbatim writer of the system, and we have no examples which suggest this, but he was certainly both accurate, consistent, and fluent. Not more than two instances have been noted where he corrected a sign or even faltered, and he very rarely writes a word in more than one, standard Gurney, way. One recalls the accuracy of another user of (Pitman) shorthand, George Bernard Shaw. However, Chinnery's penmanship varies from copybook correctness to the hastily sketchy and the latter can create problems in decipherment, particularly when it is combined with faint, erased, or incomplete signs in pen or pencil written over one hundred years ago and often not now easily legible due to the rough treatment of the sketches, and also in some cases because of Chinnery's rather odd eighteenth-century English style and vocabulary, which disturbs the help which context would otherwise lend to easy translation. However, the stage has now been reached where most of Chinnery's brief shorthand notes can be read off in immediate translation and whole sentences can be understood with ease.

One peculiar feature in Chinnery's shorthand is the use of capital letters in a way not known from the standard Gurney system, but even these are yielding to patient research. A few words or letters are still baffling and the 'stages', usually seven, used to describe his recommended procedures of theory and technique for landscape and portraits may have to remain incompletely understood unless more examples are discovered. Although the Gurney system itself may easily be studied, it seems very unlikely that it will ever be possible to compile a word-list of more than about fifteen hundred words from Chinnery's own shorthand, but even at these levels it has contributed, and will still contribute somewhat more, to a fuller appreciation of Chinnery's life and work.

The Gurney system is essentially phonetic, by syllables, as in other modern systems, though there are traces of full 'spelling' letter by letter, and nearly every letter in the alphabet has a separate sign. In the standard system (though later there were more abbreviations and spatial variations) three relative positions of adjacent signs are entirely reserved for the indication of any intermediate vowels. Initial, intermediate double, and final vowels can be additionally indicated by dots appropriately placed in the same three positions. There are a few additional rules for joining, abbreviation, and special signs, but these are mercifully few, though in Dickens' time these had been further developed, somewhat to David Copperfield's dismay.[24] The signs for consonants do not vary in significance due to thickness or position, and so the essential system consists of the signs for consonants which are either directly joined, or separately placed in one of three relative positions to indicate any vowels between them.

Chinnery's draughtsmanship and artistic style have been mentioned in comparison with that of many others; Romney, Lawrence, Hoppner, Mrs Mee, Cosway, Rowlandson, Comerford, to name only a few. Such comparative analysis is a study on its own which has hitherto been neglected and could, I think, contribute most to a true assessment of his artistic merit. But Chinnery's drawings, even without the shorthand, are immediately recognisable as his. However, some of the content of the shorthand has helped to reveal still more of the method behind his style, as well as helping to arrange them by date and subject.

In addition to the dates on the drawings there is a whole group of drawings with shorthand notes on style, colour, or draughtsmanship addressed to himself which appear frequently; others have more general remarks though usually still related in some way to the sketch; a third category consists of itemised directions for various 'stages' of drawings or painting; and a further category includes notes, again unrelated to a particular sketch, sometimes reflections on his art and sometimes merely brief notes of anniversaries, dinner-dates, references to people, etc.

Comments in the first two categories which are found frequently include the one noted above 'Picture at any time' or 'It would make an excellent picture', and also many others such as 'To fill up with pen', 'Action quite right', 'Action not quite right', 'Fully to be depended upon', 'Good and useful', 'Several studies required', 'Good', 'Excellent'. In particular cases more detailed notes are made of colours (particularly of junks, flags, clothing), the correct position of a foot, hand or head, and these can be quite detailed, for instance, 'Action not quite right, the hand should be turned to the left', or 'Several more studies required'. For a junk he noted, 'It wants a good deal of correction, particularly the head of the junk, but it is a good design. It will make by and by a pretty thing'. Two drawings exist of a fire engine in 'The East India Company's Hong, Canton' and are dated 1832, on one of which is noted 'The body of the engine is dark green. All the edges and ends of the poles are red. The wheels are red excepting the iron ends. The axletree is red'. Chinnery was clearly very exact and precise and made these notes to ensure an accurate reproduction in any later picture. Three specially interesting brief notes are 'At home', 'Monday morning', and 'Fix'. By 'At home' Chinnery was careful to note that he was re-working a drawing and not drawing 'from nature' (which he defined elsewhere as the source of the best drawings), but was 'filling up' in pen a previous quick sketch which he had done on the spot, often in pencil. Sometimes, however, he does indicate that both the initial outline and the filling up were done consecutively, and on one occasion he gives the time taken and then comments 'Breakfast well earned'. He has been recorded as fond of being out early in the day to sketch, whether to escape the heat or the crowds is not known.[25] Another almost poetic comment occurs on a sketch dated at Macao May 24, 1839, 'Nothing could exceed the beauty of the morning effect around half past six'. But at least his method seems clear in that he had a very quick overall grasp of a scene, almost like a cartoonist, and reminiscent sometimes of Gilray, Rowlandson or even Romney. He then went over this again rather than initially and laboriously perfecting each outline and part separately. His ability to fill up an initial sketch at a later date with accuracy and confidence is equally remarkable. By 'Monday morning' he seems merely to have been creating a reminder for himself in his rather remote residence in Macau, though it is just possible that there was some deeper significance in the comment. The word 'Fix' occurs frequently on his drawings and presumably notes those sketches in pencil or charcoal with which he was satisfied and wished to protect against wear and erasure. Shorthand notes on other drawings have further revealed that his method of fixing drawings was, in imitation of the then current use of hot milk for this purpose, to use Chinese congee (a rice gruel) which apparently served as a satisfactory substitute, and he notes 'congee very hot'. It has been said, however, that some such 'fixing' was 'applied to drawings to determine the possibilities as an engraving'.[26]

Apart from such shorthand notes which occur more than once or are routine comments, there are other unusual or unique notes. These occur in unexpected places and they mostly do not refer to any adjacent sketch. A small group of this sort, probably less than twenty examples, have what have been revealed to be itemised stages in the completion of a particular work, or of landscape painting, and drawing in general. These were not immediately understandable because of the use of many capital letters. Fortunately we have just a few examples where Chinnery gives, still in shorthand, the meaning of at least some of the letters. I suspected, and this has turned out to be true, that they are abbreviations for the several 'stages' which Chinnery identified in his artistic methods, sometimes further refined into 'theory' and 'practice'. Some are really quite simple, such as PO for perfect outline, FGS for full grey stage, and R & C (often written to look like RM) meaning 'repair and completion', PEP for 'perfect enriching of parts', V for 'varnish', PD for 'perfect drawing'. These identifications will soon have been taken as far as they can be unless more examples are found. In addition to being artistic directions for various types of picture, these stages are often numbered, usually from one to seven. However, the stages can be repeated out of order and instructions occur in such orders as 7234561, 23456721 and 34256. More stages than seven have also been found.

Just a few of these complicated examples in shorthand and abbreviations are quite clearly intended for, or many have formed part of, a treatise which Chinnery was working on in India as revealed by his correspondence with Mrs Browne.[27]   Unfortunately it never seems to have been published and the fact that a few pages survive is probably because they were written next to, or were mixed with, the sketches.   Other examples or pages on their own may well have been destroyed after his death when his effects were auctioned, because they were incomprehensible and had no obvious artistic merit.   This is one of the greatest losses of Chinnery research material.

One such page (not connected with any sketch) has the clear reference in shorthand, 'See page 41 opposite' and another 'see opposite page' and so it cannot be doubted that Chinnery had made considerable progress in putting down on paper the theory and practice of his art.   Even more interesting is the fact that this surviving page (presumably page 40 rather than 42, if the odd numbers were rectos) is dated 'Macau November 24 1833' and proves that Chinnery was still refining in Macau the teaching methods which he had established earlier in India.   More material may yet be rediscovered and it would certainly be the most important which we could have for understanding Chinnery's artistic philosophy and its practical application.

While lamenting the lack of such materials we can, however, still benefit from the other random notes in shorthand which are biographical, amusing, or historical records.   It is not possible here to give more than a brief selection of these.   One of the earliest examples is also particularly interesting as it shows that Chinnery apparently was commissioned to provide illustrations for Henry Fielding's last novel *Amelia*, written in 1751 and often reprinted since then.   Fielding was particularly concerned in his novel with social evils and prison conditions in Britain.   Chinnery's several illustrations for this novel were drawn prior to his departure for India in 1802.[28]   They are drawn in a style using bold enveloping pen or brush strokes which has been likened to Romney's and does occur elsewhere in a few of Chinnery's drawings.   They are, among the few or perhaps, the only surviving sketches done before he left for India.   Whether they were ever published has not yet been proved, but there is one other curious if remote link between Chinnery and Fielding.   Both are buried in Portuguese territory.   Three years after *Amelia* was published Fielding sailed to Lisbon to improve his health and died there two months later.   His grave in the British Cemetery and Chinnery's in the Protestant Cemetery in Macau are visited by many tourists.

Of the period Chinnery spent in India there are fewer surviving sketches than for the period after 1825 in Macau, Canton and Hongkong.   Presumably he left much material behind him when he left India.   But the shorthand was still used.   I have translated precise references from the Indian period which give the date he arrived in Dublin, the date of his marriage, and the date he arrived in Madras.   These confirm other references.   Other biographical remarks occur and are slightly unusual for the rather serious-minded Chinnery who, though garrulous and witty among friends, permitted himself few quips with a pencil in his hand and a sketchbook on his knee.   However, under what appears to be a resketching of a very early miniature self-portrait, he does allow himself the comment '50 years ago when I looked something like a gentleman'.   Another brief but meaningful note dated January 5, 1840 is '66 years old today!!!'.   His exclamation marks are expressive, but at least his date of birth is confirmed.[29]   In yet another instance the reading of the shorthand has confirmed another dated record.   A sketch of the Canton factories dated December 29, 1832 has the note 'Mr Marjoribanks picture taken home on the *York* January 1832'.   This corresponds with the report in the newspaper the Canton Register for January 1832 which has a notice of the farewell ceremonies for Mr Marjoribanks who was President of the Select Committee of the

East India Company and left in H. C. S. *York*.   The same paper on February 2, 1832 includes Chinnery's name as among forty-one signatories who published a congratulatory letter.[30]   Another shorthand note on a sketch of March 7, 1831 says 'the day of the races' and this links up with a description of the races on that day in Harriet Low's journal.[31]   On another occasion Chinnery, who is known to have enjoyed a late night out at Mr Jardine's, makes the comment 'Breakfasted and the whole filled up before 9.   The result of going to bed at 8'.

Several names also occur in the shorthand which read like a commentary on the times — Jardine, Dent, Matheson, Gutzlaff, George Smith, Sturgis, Caldwell, Colledge, Mrs Grant, Mrs Underwood, Alloy, Assor, and several others, but even so one could wish for still more identification in some of the sketches where people and faces occur.   But Chinnery was working for himself and his own time and much that could have been of historical interest is not given.   He does not mention anything of the stirring times in which he lived.

Two notes refer back to his early life, though they occur much later on sketches of completely unconnected subjects.   One, previously referred to as a 'reference to Romney'[32] actually reads: 'If I have one sitting or 20 I paint over the whole head at each sitting.   Romney 1798'.   It is certain that this was a reference to George Romney (his brother Peter died in 1777) and helps to confirm my surmise that Chinnery might just possibly have been his pupil.[33]   The second unusual note reads: 'Hoppner's portrait of the King when Prince of Wales for the Queen.   Not to forget'.   It is not clear to which of Hoppner's several portraits of George IV this refers.[34]

It has been said that Chinnery was most at home with miniatures and landscape but there is no doubt that he preferred to sketch 'from nature'.   It is only from a knowledge of the shorthand that we are able to read such comments as 'The best sketches are made by a very faint sketch from nature and filled up without any rubbing, i.e. filled up over the original', and again, 'It is the power of extracting the poetry from the prose of all objects in nature that constitutes the genius for both poetry and painting'.   That was written on March 24, 1849 though it has a later date added, January 20, 1852, only about four months before Chinnery died.   It is a sad thought that perhaps the perseverance and perception revealed from a translation of his shorthand was for many years hindered by failing eyesight for, in May 1844, we find a shorthand comment 'The whole filled up with pen both pages, not so bad for a blind man'.[35]   But at least the reading of his shorthand is an eye-opener to the wealth of his prolific draughtsmanship.

Where to find them

COMPETITION for wall space is severe enough to keep Chinnery's paintings – even his best – out of prime positions in most public art galleries. Even in Hongkong and Macau there are no Chinnery wings in the existing galleries, though when the Cultural Complex is built in Tsimshatsui in Kowloon this deficiency may be remedied.

In Macau, Chinnery has a street named after him and he is lucky enough to survive in a few local records and some books in the library of the Leal Senado. There are also a few sketches in the local museum. His grave in the Old Protestant Cemetery, next to the Museum, is a point of pilgrimage for Hongkong tourists, and the site of his last home, No 8 Rua Ignacio Baptista, can still be located, though the building itself no longer stands. Rua George Chinnery is a small lane at the northern end of Ignacio Baptista.

No work outlining Chinnery's major achievements would, however, be complete without some indication as to where his paintings and sketches can be found and instead of trying to list the collections in terms of size or importance – an arguable criterion anyway since there are many who prefer his sketches and water colours to his oils – it has been decided to group them in areas.

Hongkong first: The Hongkong and Shanghai Banking Corporation, with its numerous oils and four albums of sketches, has one of the biggest private collections in the world. These paintings hang in various parts of the Bank's main building. Some can be seen in the Mezzanine gallery from the main banking hall while some of the best are hanging in the board room. These include one of Mowqua, the Hong merchant in Canton as well as two outstanding portraits from his early India period – the painting of Colonel Kirkpatrick and his two Eurasian children. There is a family group described as Charles Marjoribanks and his family in Macau, though this frame title is questionable. In the Chairman's office is the fine portrait of Howqua and elsewhere there are a number of Chinnery miniatures as well as several oils from the Macau period, including a self-portrait. Many are reproduced in this book.

The Bank's collection was started by the Chief Manager in 1920-24, Mr A. G. Stephen, who bought eight Chinnery paintings including the portraits of Howqua and Mowqua, acting on the advice of the late Mr James Orange, partner in the firm of Leigh and Orange, architects and engineers. The collection grew with subsequent Chief Managers but the greater part was assembled on the advice of Dr J. R. Jones, then the Bank's legal adviser, who bought Chinnery sketches in London, Ireland and the United States. It is now one of the most important in the world.[1]

The City Museum and Art Gallery displays its Chinnerys from time to time and occasionally adds new ones to its collections.   It also draws on large private collections – such as the extensive range of Chinnery and contemporary China coast paintings owned by Dr Jones personally and by the Hongkong and Shanghai Bank – for major exhibitions.

Of the five oils in the Hongkong Government collection attributed to Chinnery, one is a view of the Praya Grande in Macau and the other, temporarily hanging in Government House, is a family group entitled Madame Pereira and her children. Additionally the Art Gallery possesses a number of Chinnery sketches among its large collections of China coast paintings built up from bequests by such people as Sir Robert Ho Tung, Sir Paul Chater, Mr Wyndham O. Law and Geoffrey Robley Sayer.[2]

The major part of the Chater collection, including a few Chinnerys, was lost during the Japanese occupation of Hongkong from 1942-45.   A full description of this collection can be found in James Orange's illustrated volume *The Chater Collection,* now out of print but recently republished in Taiwan.

The Chinnery Bar in the Mandarin Hotel contains no originals but coloured and black and white photographs of Chinnery paintings and sketches.   In this small room can be seen a more representative selection of his works than in any public place in Hongkong.

Britain: By far the most important and representative collection in private hands is owned by the Keswick family and Jardine, Matheson and Co Ltd but for the most part these are held in the homes of the Keswicks in London and Scotland and the private offices of Matheson and Co Ltd in London.   They include some of Chinnery's best-known paintings, such as *Dent's Verandah*, one of the portraits of Sir Charles and Lady D'Oyly painted in India, portraits of Sir Jamsetje Jejeebhoy painted in Canton, another of Captain Clifton, master of Jardine Matheson's famous clipper ship, *Red Rover*, and several important water-colours and sketches.[3]

Chinnery is believed to have painted a number of portraits for William Jardine and James Matheson during his years in Macau and one writer says that a tradition survives that they paid him a retainer and received a proportion of his output in return.[4]   Certainly a number of letters survive testifying to Chinnery's close relations with the firm.   When Jardine retired in 1839 and Matheson left three years later with another partner, Henry Wright, they all took back Chinnery paintings to Britain.   Had all these paintings survived, the Jardine, Matheson collection would have been easily the biggest in the world.   Many of William Jardine's collection, however, were destroyed in London during World War II and the Matheson collection is largely dispersed.   William Keswick arrived in the Far East in 1858 and he owned several works by Chinnery.   This was the beginning of the Keswick collection.   There are several pictures of his India period but by far the largest part is devoted to the Macau years.

A picture album of the Keswick collection is kept at Jardine, Matheson's offices in Hongkong and at the City Museum and Art Gallery.

In British art galleries, Chinnery's oils are poorly represented.   However one of his masterpieces, the self-portrait painted in about 1840 is now in the National Portrait Gallery just behind Trafalgar Square.

Chinnery's drawings however are well represented in British art galleries.   Pre-eminent is the collection in the Victoria and Albert Museum, the vast majority of which were bequeathed by James Orange.   This massive collection consists of seven large scrapbooks containing a total of 1195 sheets.   The cataloguing is not complete and a conservative estimate is that there are more than 10,000 drawings.[5]   There are four oils and about 16 water-colours, mainly landscapes or street scenes painted in Ireland, India, Macau and Canton, as well as two studies probably done for the self-portrait now in the National Portrait Gallery.   There is also the engraving of Dr Thomas R. Colledge by William Daniell after Chinnery.

The British Museum has two selections of drawings and there are two water-colours; one collection of seven sheets showing Indian scenes was presented by Sir Walter Trevelyan in 1871 and the remainder, mainly scenes of Macau and Canton in pencil, pen and sepia, were purchased in October, 1886.[6]

The India Office Library has two water colours and 27 sketches, all of the India period.

The Royal Society has an oil portrait of Holman, the blind traveller.

The Tate Gallery also has a drawing which is occasionally on display.

There are several oils and water-colours in private collections.

Outside of London, at the City Museum and Art Gallery in Birmingham is the J. Leslie Wright Collection, exhibited in 1965, consisting of 14 water-colours, and one oil, all from India, and four water-colours and 33 sketches of Chinese scenes.[7]

In the Scottish border town of Hawick, Roxburghshire, the Town Council owns one of the five portraits of the Earl of Minto painted by Chinnery in Calcutta. This painting was presented to the Council by the Fourth Earl in 1893 and until recently hung over the main staircase of the Municipal Building and it is to be placed on exhibition in the new Municipal Art Gallery when this is completed.

In the National Gallery of Scotland in Edinburgh there is one painting, a self-portrait, and a drawing *Portrait of an officer*. These are not on view but can usually be seen by arrangement.

There is another collection on the east coast of Scotland in private hands containing among others the only known sketch of Caroline Shillaber who married Dr Colledge in Macau.

Other Chinnery paintings and drawings have been reported in various galleries such as the National Maritime Museum at Greenwich, the City Art Gallery in Leeds, the Graves Art Gallery in Sheffield and the National Museum of Wales.

Another portrait of the Earl of Minto used to hang in the Dutch Ambassador's residence in London between 1952 and 1964 but was then returned to the Rijksmuseum in Amsterdam.

In the National Gallery of Ireland are two Macau scenes including one of the Praya Grande, but while this has been described as an exceptionally fine painting,[8] the most important oils here are of various Irish worthies painted during Chinnery's Dublin period, including his wife, Marianne, and his wife's grandmother. Others have been reported at the Royal Dublin Society and the Royal Irish Academy.

Chinnery's paintings would make excellent wall coverings for Government buildings and embassies, redolent as they are of imperial times, but while the Governor of Hongkong, Sir Murray MacLehose, recalls having a Chinnery painting of a young ensign in uniform in his office at the British Embassy in Copenhagen, the Foreign Office tells me that this is the only Chinnery in the Diplomatic Service collection.

In Europe, there are a few drawings at the Sofartsmuseet in Troense, Denmark and in Sweden there is an oil portrait of Sir Anders Ljungstedt, Swedish Consul to China, painted by Chinnery in about 1835, though the better known painting of Ljungstedt is at the Peabody Museum in Salem, Massachusetts. There is also a collection of sketches at the Geographical Society in Lisbon.

In India, a detailed survey has yet to be made of surviving Chinnery paintings but there are some at the Prince of Wales Museum of Western India at Bombay, including the original Chinnery painting of what was thought to be Sir Jamsetje Jejeebhoy, though the frame caption (not always to be relied upon) describes the subject as 'Framji Pestonji Patuck of Bombay, born

1800, died June 22, 1840. Painted from life at Canton, China in 1833. Presented by Miss S. Patuck'.[9]

At the Bombay museum are two other Chinnerys of prominent Indians.

The oil portrait of Dr Joshua Marshman, D. D. is to be found in the Serampore College, West Bengal, India. This was the painting Chinnery did during his visit to Serampore in 1823.

In Calcutta, several of Chinnery's paintings survive including two of his masterpieces from the India period, Sir Henry Russell and Sir Francis Macnaghten, which hang in the High Court where these two British judges presided. These are exceptionally large oil paintings, that of Russell measuring 112 inches by 74 inches and that of Macnaghten, 88 inches by 60 inches. The Victoria Memorial Hall has several paintings including the portrait of the Earl of Minto, presented by the 4th Countess Minto and the Fifth Earl, and a view of Calcutta, but while three others have been attributed to Chinnery one of the Nawab's Palace at Murshidabad bears the date of 1835, 10 years after he left Calcutta for Macau, and is thought to be the work of his son Henry; two others have yet to be confirmed. The Maharaja of Burdwan and Sir Prodyot Coomar Tagore possessed at one time a large collection of Chinnery's works but these have been dispersed. There is a Chinnery self-portrait at the Asiatic Society in Calcutta, as has been mentioned earlier.[10]

In Tokyo, a large collection of Chinnery's water colours and sketches are held in two volumes in the Toyo Bunko, in the outlying suburb of Honkomagome, about a half-an-hour's train ride from central Tokyo. These were formerly owned by the late Dr G. E. Morrison of Peking. One volume contains 206 pen and ink sketches and pencil sketches and the other, 39 finished water-colours and 84 sketches. The water-colours, having been kept within the albums, are among the most exciting to be seen, retaining as they do much of their original freshness and colour. There is also a lithograph, after Chinnery, of Charles Gutzlaff, and some exceptional drawings of Hongkong done in 1846.

In the United States, large numbers of Chinnery paintings in oil and water-colour and sketches can be found, mainly on the East coast though there is a beautiful oil of steps in Macau in a private collection in California.

In the Peabody Museum in Salem, are eight oils, 30 water-colours and 200 sketches. The main part of the collection was purchased in 1932 from the heirs of Augustine Heard, senior partner of Augustine Heard & Co. Three of these oils are on display and it is necessary to apply to see the other oils, water-colours and sketches. The Chinnery collection, which includes a self-portrait, Ljungstedt, Alloy, the sampan girl, and a view of the Inner Harbour of Macau and two other landscapes, is supported by additional water-colour collections by other artists, European and Chinese. The Museum also maintains an extensive photographic reference collection on Chinnery and the oil portrait of Miss Harriet Low, owned by Mrs Francesca M. Wiig, has been passed down to her grand-daughter.

In the Metropolitan Museum in New York is a self-portrait.

In the Cooper Union in New York, which is a branch of the Smithsonian, are seven sketches. At the Fogg Museum in Cambridge, Massachusetts are two pencil sketches and at Smith College there are four more as well as three exceptional sketches in the Paul Mellon collection at Yale.

The Yale University Medical Library has an exceptionally fine ink and wash picture of the Medical Missionary Society Hospital at Macau, at one time operated by Dr Peter Parker, noted medical missionary and later U.S. Minister Plenipotentiary to China.

It is impossible to survey all the paintings in private hands in the United States but apart from California, collections are known to exist in Pennsylvania and in Cambridge, Massachusetts.[11]

This survey is by no means exhaustive but it includes the names of galleries and museums in the better known and more accessible parts of the world where Chinnery's work survives. Writing to the author from Salem, Massachusetts, Mr Francis B. Lothrop, said: "The lack of public display of Chinnery's work in Hongkong, India, England, Japan, and the United States of America is regrettable. It undoubtedly accounts for the many false identifications, as comparative study material is unavailable. Chinnery's reputation will increase if this situation is remedied."

Many Chinnerys have found their way into private homes and occasionally oils and water-colours come up for sale at antique shops or auctions in London and Hongkong.

In 1973, Christie's estimated that the price range for his pictures was between £500 and £5,000, with the average between £2,000 and £3,000.[12]   But in highly inflationary times values are apt to appreciate rapidly and at a sale in Hongkong early in 1974 simple pencil and ink sketches were selling for between £100 and £500, compared with £5 and £10 about 10 years earlier.

Letters *

Letter from George Chinnery to Sir James Matheson,
by courtesy of Matheson and Co Ltd, London

Sat. Dec. 1, 1838

Mr Dear Mr. Matheson,

I need not say that on my coming home yesterday I selected the Volume of my sketches for you which you flatter me so highly by wishing to have. How gratified I am to give it to you you may suppose! knowing me as I believe you do – I *hope* you do.

But you know what my Sketchbooks are – all full – but many in each Volume, with the embryo of design – many filled in partially – and many in their completed state of pen and sepia. The Volume in question is one of my best I am happy to say, but they must be *all* so filled in before you get it, and although I say it that should not, it will be the Sketchbook of a Painter and some 50 years hence it may be interesting – here and there I'll leave one in an unfinished state that G.C. may be seen more clearly, when it may come under the eye of a Brother of the Pencil.

Today or tomorrow kindly look in on me – most happy I'll be to see you and will explain myself better – I have written your name in the Volume.

Monday I reckon on you and in this case I'll be punctual at 8½ – but at all events tomorrow I'll come and see you sometime.

Up till ½ past one at our delightful party! but I was out at 7 and got some good drawings, but business today I fear for! You are quite well I most truly hope.

Yours most sincerely,
always,
(Sgd.) Geo. Chinnery

James Matheson, Esq.

*Chinnery's spelling style, use of capital letters, punctuation and abbreviations have been preserved. Where his handwriting was not fully legible question marks have been placed after the word. Certain words underlined in the original letters have been printed in italics.

Transcript of Chinnery manuscript letter, by courtesy of the

Hongkong and Shanghai Banking Corporation

Macao – January 26th, 1848

My dear Sir,

I am afraid I am out of your good Books and Grace by my having delayed your wishes, which do me so much honor, and not having before this transmitted to you the sketches you flattered me so much by wishing to possess – my Health has been wretched for the most part since I had the pleasure to see you here; I have had the power to do but little and that only occasionally – I lay request on your indulgence to excuse me. I have understood that you intend leaving China by this steamer(?) and I take advantage of Mr. Durran's going over tomorrow morning from this to send you rather more than the number of sketches you named, to wh. you will probably not object; and it will gratify me most truly if before you embark you will give me a word or two to say how you approve of them.   Should they obtain your suffrage it will very much delight me.

I beg to have the opportunity of conveying to Genl. D'Aguilar my high respects, as well as to Mrs. D'Aguilar on your arrival home.   To your Brother I will ask the Favor of presenting him with my very kind respects and regards!   I shall not forget, you may be assured the Honor he did me while in China of very often coming to see me, at a time when my sad Health on my part, rendered his obliging attention so seasonable(?); nor the friendly conversations we held on Art in the atelier – In his travels in Europe I hope he has continued to cultivate his talent for the pencil and for modelling(?) which held out so much promise; and wh. in the Countries he has been in it will be so much felt and appreciated – In China art may be said to be a dead letter!   Old age has lately crept on me sadly – I am over my 74th year!   but I am not without some(?)   Hope that I *may* yet be where Art is known, felt and appreciated.   I beg you will include my great respects in the assurance of being, my dear Sir,

Yours very sincerely and obliged,

Geo. Chinnery

Letter to R. J. Gilman

Macao – Saturday

25 Feby. 1848 –

My dear Mr. Gilman

I take advantage of Mr Durran's going over to Hong Kong to send under his care, which I can be sure of, the Picture of the little Tanka I have had the pleasure to paint for you; as also the Sketch Book I have made up for you – It will be a real Gratification to me should you approve of both –

My heartiest & best wishes wait on you & your intended journey home – To your Sister & Brother, pray make my most respectful & kindest Regards – I hope Mrs. Gilman continues her drawing – She is among the fin[e] specimens of the art –

If you were remaining here of course I should not hint a[t] so prosaical circumstance; but the case is, you may perhaps w[ish] to remunerate me – kindly then send me 150 Sp Dollars – 100 for Book & 50 for the Picture – & if you will allow it to be paid *here* I shall be the more obliged –

I repeat my cordial good wishes; & hoping to live to see you back again I am
My dear Mr Gilman

Yours very sincerely

& truly obliged

Geo. Chinnery

If you can permit your remittance to me to be a Draft in my favor on our friend Mr DuPaiva here, it will much increase my obligation –

Macao – February 20th, 1848.

My dear Sir,

Mr. Durran (?) called on me as your note to me of the 7th inst. stated he would do – and he explained to me your wishes regarding the alteration you proposed for me to make in the sketch I had the honor to forward to you on the 27th of last month.

Unfortunately I in the first instance misunderstood your desire in regard to the Drawings altogether – it never occurred to me that you were anxious to have views &c of Hong Kong – I thought your flattering commission to me in August last had reference to those of my sketches which I had made in China (speaking generally) – Had I understood your wishes in the first instance, I should have explained to you how very sincerely I regret that *at this moment* it is out of my power to replace those sketches. I have removed at your request, from the volume of(?) others which I made at Hong Kong in 1846 – I was there 6 months only; at the time so very unwell, not to say ill, that I had the power of doing but very little; and those views I made there I have commissions to execute Pictures from for particular parties whose names are written for the most part *in their own hand writing* on the several pages of the respective sketches.

It will therefore be evident to you my dear Sir that I have not the power of parting with these – but I will with very great pleasure make you copies of any of the Views I have of the town of Victoria and transmit them to you by the May mail, if you will have the goodness to leave with Mr. Wilkinson Dent, directions where to forward them to you in England. I have in all but 15 (Fifteen) views – and of these I now enclose you a list. – they are large and full of detail – any of those you will point out, I will be most happy to prepare for you by the time I mention. The native population, the costume, Junks, Boats &c are the same which are seen throughout the Country.

I have removed the figures you wished and have added others in their stead; they all apply to this country (to China speaking generally) for all the sketches. I have (exclusive of the views I made at Hong Kong) more made either here or at Canton – and they were all done from nature.

I wish you particularly to understand, that if the little Collection I now have the pleasure to forward to you does not answer your wishes or expectations, that you will for a moment think you are under any obligation to retain it. – and if you will return it to me through Mr. Wilkinson Dent, and write me, pointing out the views of Hong Kong you think will meet your wishes I should be only too happy to execute them and exchange them for the present Volumes. – but they are large and comprise great detail; and with reference to the time they will employ me I should be only able to convey to you 6 as an equivalent for those in the present collection. – if on the other hand you wish me to extend the number of the Drawings I will forward to Mr. W. Dent (if you so permit me) my account for as many as I may complete at your request. I say this to prevent any misunderstanding at a future period.

My most(?) respectful compliments wait on General(?) D'Aguilar and I remain,

My dear sir,

Yours very faithfully,

Geo. Chinnery

Capt. D'Aguilar,

162

Notes and references

Foreword

1. Berry-Hill, Henry and Sidney, *George Chinnery, 1774-1852, Artist of the China Coast,* F. Lewis, Publishers Ltd, Leigh-on-Sea, England.
2. Geoffrey W. Bonsall, Director, Hongkong University Press in a letter to the author.
3. Sir William Foster, *British Artists in India, 1760-1820,* Vol XIX, 1930-31
4. Francis B. Lothrop, Hon. Trustee, Peabody Museum, Salem, Mass. U.S.A.

Chapter 1.

1. W. H. Welply, *Cork Historical and Archaeological Society Journal,* Vol XXXVII, 1933. This book is mentioned and illustrated in *English Handwriting, 1540-1853,* by Joyce Irene Whalley, London, HMSO, 1969.
2. Bovill, E. W. *Notes and Queries,* 1954, quoting from *Benezit,* the dictionary of artists.
3. See Note 29 in the chapter on *George Chinnery's shorthand* in this book.
4. Anthony Pasquin, writing in *A Liberal Critique on the Present Exhibition of the Royal Academy* in 1794, and quoted by Welply.
5. Richard Ormond, in *A Catalogue of Irish Portraits 1660-1860* and Walter G. Strickland in *A Dictionary of Irish Artists.*
6. such as Welply.
7. in the *Dictionary of National Biography*
8. Bovill
9. Bovill and Welply
10. an anonymous Irish critic quoted by Bovill
11. Bovill
12. Graham Reynolds in *English Portrait Miniatures,* A & C Black, 1952
13. Welply
14. Ibid.
15. Ibid.
16. Berry-Hill
17. Ibid. Prominently displayed on the palette is the hallmark "E" (for the year 1800-01) and the maker's mark.
18. Strickland
19. Ibid.
20. Berry-Hill
21. Bovill
22. J. R. Jones
23. Ibid.
24. The Times, London, March 21, 1961
25. J. R. Jones

26. Welply. There is an echo of William Chinnery's days as Agent General for N.S.W. in London, in the Mitchell Library in Sydney. In the correspondence of Captain John Piper there is a reference to missing arrears of salary, paid from London in those days. A Captain J. Foveaux, who like Piper served as Lt. Governor of Norfolk Island, off the N.S.W. coast, in the early part of the 19th century and later retired, wrote that "Chinnery was a damn rascal and kept everything and the money to himself." This was dated January 24, 1812.

27. J. R. Jones

28. Welply

29. Ibid.

Chapter II

1. Brian Gardner, *The East India Company,* Rupert Hart Davis, London, 1971

2. F. B. Lothrop

3. Gardner

4. Cotton, J.J., *Bengal Past and Present, Vol XXVII*

5. Ibid.

6. Ibid.

7. such as Lothrop, Jones and Ormond

8. Lothrop

9. such as Lothrop

10. Berry-Hill

11. Sir William Foster makes this claim but so far no confirmation has come to light.

12. Cotton. It is now the National Library.

13. Contemporary account quoted by Cotton

14. Madras Courier

15. Foster

16. by Bovill among others

17. Bovill

18. such as Berry-Hill

19. Ibid.

20. W. C. Hunter, *Bits of Old China.*

Chapter III

1. J. J. Cotton

2. Berry-Hill

3. G. W. Bonsall in a letter to the author.

4. Allan Carr, in the foreword to the catalogue of the Arts Council Exhibition, London and Edinburgh, 1957

5. Mildred Archer: *The talented Baronet: Sir Charles D'Oyly and his drawings of India,* The Connoisseur, London

6. Ibid.

7. Ibid.

8. Ibid.

9. *Bengal Past and Present* Vol 35.

10. Calcutta Chronicle, March 9, 12 and 14, (quoted by Sir William Foster)

11. from Alexander's East India Magazine, (quoted by Foster)

12. Foster

13. Calcutta Monthly Journal of August 1837, pp 569 and 579

14. Cotton

15. Ibid

16. *Tom Raw the Griffin,* Sir Charles D'Oyly, R. Ackermann, London, 1828.

17. Chinnery was clearly a great admirer of Reynold's work. In the next chapter he refers in a letter to a pupil to Sir Joshua's "admirable and never enough to be admired lectures."

18. Berry-Hill
19. W. C. Hunter

Chapter IV

1. Richard Ormond, *George Chinnery and his pupil,* Mrs Browne, The Walpole Society, 1974
2. Ibid.
3. Mildred Archer
4. Richard Ormond
5. Ibid.
6. Ibid.
7. Ibid. This treatise together with some of the letters, was purchased by Mr Paul Mellon, some years ago at auction. When Mr Mellon discovered that the British Museum owned the other half of the same batch of letters he kindly donated his half to the Museum. Mr Mellon retained the treatise in the form of a notebook with sketches by Chinnery and made available copies to Mr Francis Lothrop and Richard Ormond and it is Mr Ormond's transcription that the Walpole Society published in 1974.

Chapter V

1. Michael Edwardes, *British India,* Sidgwick and Jackson, 1967
2. Sir William Foster
3. J. J. Cotton, in *Bengal Past and Present.*
4. Grant Duff (See Page 702 Modern India, Part III, *An Advanced History of India,* Majumdar, Raychaudhuri and Datta, London, 1951)
5. Calcutta Govt Gazette, June 27, 1816, quoted by Foster, and it was also the Calcutta Govt Gazette of November 30, 1815 which reported Chinnery's design for the transparency celebrating the victory at Waterloo.
6. Foster
7. Ibid.
8. Ibid.
9. Ibid.
10. Calcutta Govt Gazette of June 16, 1828.
11. Foster
12. Berry-Hill, quoting from Sir Edward Paget's personal papers. The portrait survives in the family home in England.
13. Cotton
14. Berry-Hill quoting from Vigée Lebrun: *Life Works and Friendships,* W. H. Helm, London
15. Bovill
16. Bovill.
17. His brother, John, a senior merchant of the East India Company, suffered from mental infirmities and died in 1817, and it could have been John Chinnery's initial illness that William Hickey heard of in London and assumed that it was George who was stricken.
18. Richard Ormond
19. Bovill.
20. J. R. Jones
21. Bovill
22. Ibid.
23. Foster
24. Cotton
25. Miss Margaret Goldney, who supervises the Hongkong and Shanghai Banking Corporation collection recalls that at a recent sale in London, a Chinnery pencil sketch of William Locker in uniform standing by his horse (with hindquarters facing the artist) was put up for sale. There was a note attached to the picture, presumably written by Locker's son, describing how Chinnery had charged £105 for the portrait, and that he believed he had gone to China heavily in debt, and had given William Locker an

album of drawings as a contribution towards redeeming a debt of £300.   Locker's regiment, the 8th Light Dragoons, was in India from 1802-1822.   He held the rank of Captain before going on half-pay in 1819.

26.   W. C. Hunter in *Bits of Old China*
27.   Miss Harriet Low.

Chapter VI

1.   J. J. Cotton quoting Mr John Clark Marshman.
2.   Letter from F. B. Lothrop to the author.
3.   Richard Ormond.
4.   Allan Carr in the Foreword to the Catalogue of the Arts Council Exhibition, London and Edinburgh.
5.   Carl Crossman, in *The China Trade*, The Pyne Press, Princeton, U.S.A.
6.   Rex and Thea Rienits, in *The Voyages of Captain Cook,* Paul Hamlyn, London.
7.   Graham Reynolds
8.   Carl Crossman
9.   Ibid.
10.   Ibid.
11.   Sir William Foster

Chapter VII

1.   Maurice Collis, *Raffles,* Faber and Faber, 1966
2.   William Gaunt in The Times of Nov 30, 1965
3.   Harriet Low: *My Mother's Journal, 1829-1834,* Katherine Hillard, Boston, 1900, the original manuscript of which is in the Library of Congress, Washington, D.C.
4.   Buckminster was a famous Unitarian minister in the U.S.A. but Mr Francis Lothrop whose great great grandfather, also a minister, married Buckminster's sister writes that his sermons "seem dreadfully dull today".
5.   The Peabody Museum in Salem, Mass., owned a pencil sketch with colour notes of Mr Beale's bird of paradise.
6.   The Canton Register of 1832 reported that 27 inches of rain fell in two days in June of that year.

Chapter VIII

1.   The Rev. G. N. Wright, *China, in a series of views,* Fisher, Son & Co, London 1843
2.   Richard Ormond, in *George Chinnery and the Keswick family,* The Connoisseur, London
3.   W. C. Hunter in *Bits of Old China*
4.   Ibid.
5.   Letter by S. P. Fearon to Sunday Post Herald, June 1974
6.   F. B. Lothrop in a letter to the author
7.   S. P. Fearon's letter to Sunday Post-Herald
8.   Richard Ormond in *George Chinnery's Image of Himself.*   The Connoisseur, London.
9.   Ibid.
10.   W. C. Hunter.
11.   Ibid.
12.   Richard Ormond, in *George Chinnery and the Keswick Family.*
13.   Ibid.
14.   in *Bits of Old China.*
15.   Canton Register, Dec. 8 1835.
16.   Sir Lindsay Ride, *Robert Morrison,* HK University Press, 1957.
17.   Ibid.

18. Albert Ten Eyck Gardner, *Cantonese Chinnerys, Portrait of Howqua and other Chinese Trade Paintings,* The Arts Quarterly, Detroit Institute of Arts, 1953.
19. *The Fan Kwae in Canton,* Kegan Paul Trench and Co London, 1882.
20. Gardner.

Chapter IX

1. Lt Col. S. P. Fearon's letter to Sunday Post-Herald, June, 1974.
2. Luis Gomes, Curator of the Museum Luis de Camoens.
3. Capt Arthur Cunynghame, *An Aide de Camp's Recollections of Service in China,* 2 vols, Saunders and Otley, London, 1844.
4. Carl Crossman's *The China Trade.*
5. Ibid.
6. *China and the Chinese,* by Henry Charles Sirr, Wm. S. Orr, London, 1849.
7. M. La Vollée in L'Artiste, Revue de Paris, 1849, quoted by Gardner.
8. Crossman.
9. *China and the Chinese* by Henry Charles Sirr, Wm S. Orr, London, 1849.
10. C. Toogood Downing *The Fan-qui in China in 1836-37,* three vols, Henry Colburn, London.
11. Soame Jenyns, Former Deputy keeper of Oriental Antiquaries, British Museum, in a lecture on Chinnery at the Hongkong University, March 16, 1974.
12. Sirr.
13. Cunynghame.
14. *La Chine Ouverte* by "Old Nick", H. Fournier, Paris, 1845, quoted by Crossman.
15. Luis Gomes, Curator of the Museum Luis de Camoens.
16. *History of a Portrait,* by Capt Robert Bennet Forbes, by kind permission of the Museum of the American China Trade, Milton, Massachusetts, U.S.A.
17. Prof. E. V. Gulick, in *Peter Parker and the Opening of China,* Harvard University Press, 1973. Dr Parker became the first foreign doctor to train Chinese medical students, according to Prof. Gulick, and his senior and most distinguished "graduate" was Kwan A-to who not only successfully operated for cataracts and removed tumours but was left to run Parker's hospital in Canton for six months in 1844. His success as a physician and surgeon is testified by the fact that "apparently no abatement of the flow of patients to the hospital took place" according to Prof. Gulick. Not only did Kwan display good practical and theoretical knowledge but Parker was proud of his "talents, address, correct moral character and success as an oculist and surgeon."
18. Chinese Repository, Vol 11 May, 1834-April, 1835.
19. Carl Crossman's *The China Trade.*
20. E. V. Gulick.
21. Luis Gomes, Curator, Museum Luis de Camoens.
22. Francis Lothrop in a letter to the author.
23. Soame Jenyns.
24. Albert Ten Eyck Gardner, The Art Quarterly No 4, 1953, Detroit Institute of Arts.
25. M. La Vollee, in L'Artiste, Revue de Paris, 1849.

Chapter X

1. Harriet Low: *My Mother's Journal,* Katherine Hillard.
2. Richard Ormond and Francis Lothrop in letters to the author.
3. Francis Lothrop in a letter to the author.
4. Maurice Collis in *Foreign Mud.*
5. Ibid.
6. Berry-Hill.
7. J. R. Jones in a letter to the author.

8. W. C. Hunter in *Bits of Old China.*
9. Ibid.
10. Berry-Hill.
11. Confirmed by the author at the General Register Office, London.

Chapter XI

1. G. B. Endacott, *A History of Hongkong,* Oxford, 1964.
2. *Memoirs of the Blind Traveller,* Lt James Holman R. N., London, 1834.
3. Letter from Sir Harry Parker quoted by Maurice Collis in *Foreign Mud.*
4. Collis.
5. Ibid.
6. Catalogue of the Peabody Museum, Salem, Massachusetts, U.S.A.
7. Vol III May 1834-April 1835.
8. Richard Ormond in *George Chinnery and the Keswick Family,* The Connoisseur, London.
9. Ibid.
10. Ibid.
11. Permission to reproduce from this manuscript has been granted by the Trustees of the Museum of the American China Trade, Milton, Massachusetts, U.S.A.
12. Catalogue of the Exhibition held by the City Museum and Art Gallery, Hongkong, 1965.

Chapter XII

1. W. C. Hunter in *Bits of Old China,* published by Kegan Paul Trench & Co, 1855. The words "poco, poco" used by Chinnery are Portuguese meaning "little by little".
2. The late Mr L. C. Duke, quoted by Soame Jenyns in his Hongkong lecture on Chinnery, March 16, 1974.
3. Richard Ormond in *George Chinnery's Image of Himself,* The Connoisseur, London.
4. Ibid.
5. Published in London in 1924 and since reprinted in Taiwan.
6. Richard Ormond in *George Chinnery's Image of Himself,* The Connoisseur, London.
7. Letter from the Scottish National Gallery to the author.
8. Letter from the Secretary and Curator, Victoria Memorial Hall, Calcutta.
9. Art Union Vol VIII (1846) London.
10. Richard Ormond in *George Chinnery's Image of Himself,* The Connoisseur, London.

Chapter XIII

1. Maurice Collis, in *Foreign Mud.*
2. Christopher Hibbert in *The Dragon Wakes,* Longman, 1970.
3. Collis.
4. W. C. Hunter in *The Fan Kwae in Canton.*
5. Clagette Blake in *Charles Elliot, R N 1801-1875,* Cleaver Hume, London, 1960.
6. Maurice Collis.
7. E. J. Eitel, *Europe in China,* Kelly and Walsh, Hongkong 1895.
8. *Foreign Mud.*
9. Eitel.
10. Ibid.
11. Ibid.
12. Austin Coates, *Prelude to Hongkong,* Routledge and Kegan Paul, 1966.
13. Ibid.
14. I am indebted to Mr Geoffrey Bonsall for the discovery and translation of Chinnery's shorthand and his discovery in the Chinese Repository, Vol 9, June, 1840, Issue 2 of the arrival of the steamer *Madagascar.*

The build-up of the British fleet and the role of the East India Company steamers, aided by the Nemesis, is described in Captain W. H. Hall's *Narrative of the Voyages and services of the Nemesis from 1840 to 1843*, Henry Colburn, London, 1844.

15. *Points and Pickings:* Information about China and the Chinese, Anonymously written and published, Grant and Griffith, London, 1844.
16. F. B. Lothrop in a letter to the author.
17. Ibid.
18. G. W. Bonsall in a letter to the author.
19. Qu Zhi-ren, *The Hongkong Bank Group's Art Collection,* Arts of Asia, March/April 1971.
20. G. W. Bonsall in a letter to the author.
2 1. South China Morning Post, June 1, 1974.

Chapter XIV

1. Letter to the Sunday Post-Herald, March, 1974.   From Professor D. Evans, Hongkong University.
2. by G. W. Bonsall.
3. in *Bits of Old China.*
4. *The Morning of My Life in China,* privately printed, Canton, 1873.
5. Ibid.
6. Albert Ten Eyck Gardner.
7. The Celestial Empire, July 29, 1876.
8. Bovill.

Epilogue

1. Questions posed by the Curator of the City Museum and Art Gallery, Hongkong, Mr John Warner in his foreword to the Exhibition of Chinnery's paintings in 1965.
2. Richard Ormond.
3. Ibid.

Where to find them

1. Qu Zhi-ren, *The Hongkong Bank Group's Art Collection,* Arts of Asia, Hongkong, March/April 1971.
2. John Warner, Curator, City Museum and Art Gallery.
3. Richard Ormond, *George Chinnery and the Keswick Family,* The Connoisseur, London.
4. Ibid.
5. Francis B. Lothrop, in a letter to the author.   V & A catalogue.
6. British Museum catalogue.
7. Francis B. Lothrop in a letter to the author.
8. Ibid.
9. Geoffrey Bonsall, in a letter to the author.
10. N. R. Roy, Curator of the Victoria Memorial Museum, Calcutta, in a letter to the author.
11. The information on the whereabouts of Chinnery paintings in the U.S. was provided by Mr Francis B. Lothrop.
12. Letter from Christie's.

Notes and references on
George Chinnery's Shorthand

1. Her manuscript diary about Macao is in the Library of Congress and well described in Arthur W. Hummel, *'The journal of Harriet Low'*, U.S. Library of Congress, Quarterly Journal of Current Acquisitions, vol. 2, nos. 3 and 4, 1945, pp. 45-60.

2. In the collection of the Peabody Museum, Salem, Mass. Drawing no. M 13695a.

3. His letter of Saturday December 1, 1838 to James Matheson indicates this possibility. That he collected his sketches, possibly each year, is well attested by the number of drawings on which, for instance, he wrote in longhand 'Sketches in Macao 1839' in the style of a title page for that year's collection. (See also James Orange, *'George Chinnery: pictures of Macao and Canton'*, Studio, 94, 1927, p. 239. Orange notes title-pages or vignettes for 1825, 1826, 1832, 1836, and 1839). It seems very likely that Chinnery had in mind the publication of at least some of these volumes, although he was probably forced to collect them in some way in order to control his prolific output. Auguste Borget who met Chinnery and lived for several months in Macao, and Chinnery's good friend there W.W. Wood both published volumes of their sketches and it may be that Chinnery would have liked to do the same if he had had the contacts and the money. Besides these title-pages there are a few other examples of Chinnery's longhand on the sketches.

4. I am particularly grateful to Miss Margaret Goldney for arranging for me to consult this extensive collection of sketches now arranged in bound volumes.

5. Listed in the Library's *Catalogue of the Asiatic Library of Dr G. E. Morrison. Part first.: English Books.* Tokyo, Oriental Library, 1924, p. 168.

6. I am grateful to Mr Francis B. Lothrop and Dr J. R. Jones for access to a microfilm of the drawings in this collection.

7. Both museums kindly arranged for the photographing of their collections.

8. Mentioned in C. A. Montalto de Jesus, *'George Chinnery,'* China journal, VIII, no. 6, June 1928, p. 296.

9. The Hongkong and Shanghai Banking Corporation has a small sketchbook in which the shorthand has been erased.

10. See the catalogue of the exhibition at the Peabody Museum, Salem, *George Chinnery (1774-1852) and other artists of the Chinese scene, June 15 – September 15, 1967*, p. xi and the translations in the catalogue entries.

11. See Richard L. Ormond, *'George Chinnery's image of himself, Part I.'* The Connoisseur, v. 167, February 1968, p. 92.

12. See E. W. Bovill, *'George Chinnery (1774-1852)'*, Notes and Queries, n.s.1, May 1954, p. 214, note 2. Bovill attributes the identification of the shorthand to Mr William J. Carlton (see below, note 16) and quotes Sir Charles D'Oyly's reference to 'notes of shorthand.'

13. W. H. Gurney Salter, *A history of the Gurney system of shorthand.* Oxford, Blackwell, 1924, p. 10.

14. Cf. Exhibition catalogue, *George Chinnery 1774-1852*, Hongkong, City Hall Art Gallery, 1st March to 28th April 1965, p. 11.

15. The *British Museum Catalogue* lists an 18th edition of 1884.

16. Mr Carlton, who died in 1971 was still assisting in the study of Chinnery's shorthand until 1970 when aged over 80. According to Mr Carlton the collection comprises 'something like 14,000 items on stenography and kindred subjects'.

17. Gurney Salter, *History,* p. 15.

18. Private letter of 19 November 1969 from Alan R. Kennedy of W. B. Gurney and Sons.

19. Gurney Salter, *History*, p. 11.

20. Thos. Gurney, *Brachygraphy* . . . sixth edition, 1767. On pp. 47-8, there is a list of users of the system who presumably subscribed for that edition. The first entry is 'William Chinnery, Junior. Writing-Master and Accomptant, in Gough Square, who for his own private use has wrote in this method the Book of Psalms, and the New Testament. (Vide Page 35.)'. I am especially grateful to the late W. J. Carlton for the gift of a copy of this rare 1767 sixth edition.

21. See Peabody Museum, *George Chinnery (1774-1852) and other artists of the Chinese scene*, p. 12, no. 95 and note 28 below.

22. William Chinnery was the author of a popular book first published in 1750, *Writing and drawing made easy, amusing and instructive*. See Joyce Irene Whalley, *English handwriting, 1540-1853: an illustrated survey based on material in the National Art Library, Victoria and Albert Museum*. London, HMSO, 1969, p. 62.

23. William J. Carlton, *Charles Dickens, shorthand writer. The 'prenctice days of a master craftsman*. London, Palmer, 1926, ch. 2, 'Taming the stenographic shrew', pp. 31-45, and pp. 141-144.

24. Carlton, *Charles Dickens, shorthand writer*, pp. 32 and 34. 'When I had groped my way blindly, through these difficulties, and had mastered the alphabet, which was an Egyptian Temple in itself, there then appeared a procession of new horrors called arbitrary characters; the most despotic characters I have ever known; who insisted, for instance, that a thing like the beginning of a cobweb, meant expectation, and that a pen and ink sky-rocket stood for disadvantageous. When I had fixed these wretches in my mind, I found that they had driven everything else out of it; then, beginning again, I forget them; while I was picking them up, I dropped the other fragments of the system; in short, it was almost heart-breaking'.

25. Harriet Low confirms his fondness for breakfast and early rising. See Peabody Museum, *George Chinnery (1774-1852) and other artists of the Chinese scene*, p. 3, no. 6.

26. Peabody Museum, *George Chinnery (1774-1852) and other artists of the Chinese scene*, p. 7, no. 44.

27. R. L. Ormond, *'Chinnery and his pupil Mrs Browne'*, Walpole Society, Vol. XLIV, 1972-74.

28. Some of these drawings, which were brought to my attention by Mr Francis Lothrop, appear to have the date 1800. See above, note 21.

29. January 7, 1774 has been given by some writers and, like many 'facts' about Chinnery's life, has been copied by others. It seems unlikely that Chinnery would have made a mistake on this, though W. H. Welply does quote the St. Bride's Church registers as giving January 7, 1774. See W. H. Welply, *'George Chinnery, 1774-1852, with some account of his family and genealogy'*, Cork Historical and Archaeological Society Journal, vol. XXXVII, 1932, p. 13.

30. This newspaper exists in the University of Hongkong Library.

31. Mr F. B. Lothrop pointed out to me the entry on this date in the manuscript diary.

32. Exhibition catalogue by Arts Council Gallery, *George Chinnery 1774-1852*. London, 1957, entry 91.

33. Chinnery left for Ireland at about the time that Romney's health failed. Both wished to be free of portraiture, both were reluctant to finish paintings, both were rather eccentric characters, and both lived apart from their wives.

34. One wonders whether there is some connection here with the King's portrait which hung in the East India Company premises at Canton and was later brought to Hongkong, though that one is said to have been painted by Sir Thomas Lawrence.

35. Julian James Cotton in *'George Chinnery, Artist (1774-1852)'*, Bengal past and present, vol. XXVII, pp. 115 and 122 in mentioning miniature portraits quotes Sir Charles D'Oyly's note to canto V of *Tom Raw the griffin:* 'Mr C. originally practised in miniature, but nature alarmed at his prototypic progress and fearing he would come up to her, robbed him of one of his visual organs and rendered the other too weak to admit of his following this branch of his art'. I have not previously taken this very seriously and nor, it seems, has anyone else. But reconsidering Chinnery's self-portraits with this remark in mind one is faced with the striking possibility that Chinnery was indeed going blind in his left eye which is usually, though not always, deeply shaded and in several cases is represented as a mere blur. It is surprising that of his contemporaries only D'Oyly mentions his eyesight so precisely, but Chinnery is known to have had trouble with his eyes while in India and the self-portraits are very strong evidence. Perhaps this is why the other eye seems so penetrating.

Bibliography

Archer, Mildred, *The talented baronet: Sir Charles D'Oyly and his drawings of India,* The Connoisseur, London, November, 1970.

Berry-Hill, Henry and Sidney, *George Chinnery, 1774-1852,* F. Lewis, Leigh-on-Sea, 1963.

Blake, Clagette, *Charles Elliot, R. N.* 1801-1875, Cleaver-Hume, London, 1960.

Bovill, E. W., *George Chinnery (1774-1852),* Notes and Queries, Vol. 1, 5 and 6, 1954.

Coates, Austin, *Prelude to Hongkong,* Routledge & Kegan Paul, London, 1966.

Collis, Maurice, *Foreign Mud,* Faber and Faber, London, 1946.

Collis, Maurice, *Wayfoong,* Faber and Faber, 1965.

Cotton, Julian James, *George Chinnery,* Bengal: Past and Present, Vol. XXVII.

Crossman, Carl, *The China Trade,* The Pyne Press, Princeton, 1972.

Cunynghame, Capt. Arthur, *An Aide de Camp's Recollections of Service in China,* 2 vols, Saunders and Otley, London, 1844.

Downing, C. Toogood, *The Fan-qui in China in 1836-7,* 3 vols, Henry Colburn, London.

Edwardes, Michael, *British India,* Sidgwick and Jackson Ltd., 1967.

Eitel, E. J., *Europe in China,* Kelly & Walsh, 1895.

Endacott, G. B. *A History of Hongkong,* Oxford, London, 1964.

Foster, Sir William, *British Artists in India,* 1760-1820, Vol XIX, 1930-31, Oxford, 1931.

Gardner, Albert Ten Eyck, *Portraits of Howqua and other Chinese Trade Paintings,* The Arts Quarterly, Detroit Institute of Arts, 1953.

Gardner, Brian *The East India Company,* Rupert Hart Davis, London, 1971.

Griffiths, Sir Percival, *The British Impact on India,* Macdonald, London, 1952.

Gulick, Edward, V. *Peter Parker and the Opening of China,* Harvard University Press, Cambridge, Massachusetts, U.S.A., 1973.

Gutzlaff, Charles, *Journal of Three Voyages along the coast of China in 1831, 1832 and 1833,* Frederick Westley and A. H. Davis, London, 1834.

Hall, W. H., *Narrative of the Voyages and Services of the Nemesis from 1840 to 1843,* Henry Colburn, London, 1844.

Hibbert, Christopher, *The Dragon Wakes,* Longmans Green and Co., Ltd., London, 1969.

Hickey, William, *Memoirs 1745-1809,* Hurst and Blackett, London.

Holman, Lt James, *Memoirs of the Blind Traveller,* London, 1834.

Hunter, W. C., *Bits of Old China,* Kegan Paul Trench and Co., London, 1855.

Hunter, W. C., *The Fan Kwae at Canton,* Kegan Paul Trench and Co., London, 1882.

Jenyns, Soame, *George Chinnery,* lecture delivered at Hongkong University, March 16, 1974.

Mackenzie, Compton, *Realms of Silver,* Routledge and Kegan Paul Ltd., London, 1954.

Montalto de Jesus, C. A., *George Chinnery,* China Journal Vol. VIII No. 6, June, 1928.

Morrison: *Memoirs of the life and labours of Robert Morrison, D.D.,* compiled by his widow, 2 vols, Longmans, Orme, Brown Green and Longmans, 1839.

Nye, Gideon, *The Morning of My Life in China,* Privately Printed, Canton 1873.

Orange, James, *The Chater Collection,* London, 1924.

Orange, James, *Chinnery in China,* The Studio, Vol. XCIV No. 415, October, 1927.

Ormond, Richard, *George Chinnery and the Keswick family,* The Connoisseur, London, December, 1970.

Ormond, Richard, *George Chinnery and his pupil,* Mrs. Browne, The Walpole Society, 1974.

Ormond, Richard, *George Chinnery's image of himself,* Parts I and II, The Connoisseur, London, February, March, 1968.

Qu Zhi-ren, *The Hongkong Bank Group's Art Collection,* Arts of Asia, Hongkong, March/April 1971.

Reischauer, Fairbank and Craig, *East Asia, The Modern Transformation,* George Allen and Unwin Ltd, London, Vol. II, 1965.

Reynolds Graham, *British Artists Abroad, Alexander and Chinnery in China,* Geographical Magazine, Vol. XX, No. 5, 1947.

Reynolds Graham, *English Portrait Miniatures,* A. & C. Black, London, 1952.

Ride, Lindsay, *Robert Morrison,* Hongkong University Press, 1957.

Rienits, Rex and Thea, *The Voyages of Captain Cook,* Paul Hamlyn, London, 1968.

Ryan, Thomas F., *Jesuits in China,* Catholic Truth Society, Hongkong, 1964.

Sirr, Henry Charles, *China and the Chinese,* Wm. S. Orr, London, 1849.

Spencer, Alfred: *Memoirs of William Hickey,* Vol. IV (1790-1809), Hurst & Blackett, Ltd., London.

Strickland, Walter G., *A Dictionary of Irish Artists,* Vol. I, Maunsel & Co., Ltd., Dublin, 1913.

Teixeira, Fr Manuel, *Chinnery,* Noticias de Macau, 1974.

Teixeira, Fr Manuel, *George Chinnery,* Imprensa Nacional, Macau, 1974 (in Portuguese).

Vinacke, Harold, *A History of the Far East in Modern Times,* George Allen and Unwin, London, 1950.

Welply, W. H. *George Chinnery,* 1774-1852, *with some account of his family and genealogy,* Cork Historical and Archaeological Society Journal Vol. XXXVII, 1932 and Notes and Queries, Vol. 152, Nos. 2, 3 and 4, 1927.

Wright, the Rev. G. N., *China, in a series of views,* Fisher, Son & Co., London, 1843.

Catalogues:

Arts Council Exhibition, Edinburgh and London, 1957.

British Museum, London.

City Museum and Art Gallery exhibition, Birmingham, 1965.

City Museum and Art Gallery exhibition, Hongkong, 1965.

Ho-tung Collection, Hongkong, 1959.

Hongkong and Shanghai Banking Corporation Collection, Hongkong.

Keswick Collection, a private photograph album, Jardine, Matheson & Co., Ltd.

Museum Luis de Camoens, Macau, 1974.
National Portrait Gallery, London.
Paintings from the Government Collection, Hongkong, 1962.
Peabody Museum exhibition, Salem, Massachusetts, USA, 1967.
Tate Gallery exhibition, London, 1932.
Victoria and Albert Museum, London.

Correspondence and Interviews:

Bonsall, Mr Geoffrey, Hongkong, November 1973-1974.
Goldney, Miss Margaret, Hongkong, 1973-1974.
Gomes, Mr. Luis, G. Macau, 1974.
Jones, Dr. J. R., Hongkong, May-December, 1973.
Lothrop, Mr. F. B., Salem, Massachusetts, 1973-1974.
Ormond, Mr. Richard, London, May-December, 1973.
Teixeira, Fr. M., Macau, 1973-1974.
Warner, Mr. John, Hongkong, 1973-1974.

Newspapers:

Bengal Hurkaru, 1852.
Canton Register, December 8, 1835.
Celestial Empire, July 29, 1876.
Chinese Recorder and Missionary Journal, November 1887.
Chinese Repository, Vol. II, May, 1834-April 1835 and Vol. IX, June 1840.
Friend of China and Hongkong Gazette, June 1852.
Friend of India, July 8, 1852.
Financial Times, London, 1973.
Hongkong Register, September 1, 1845, Jan-December, 1852.
South China Morning Post 1930-1974.
Sunday Post-Herald, Jan-March, 1974.
The Times, London, 1946-1974.

Index

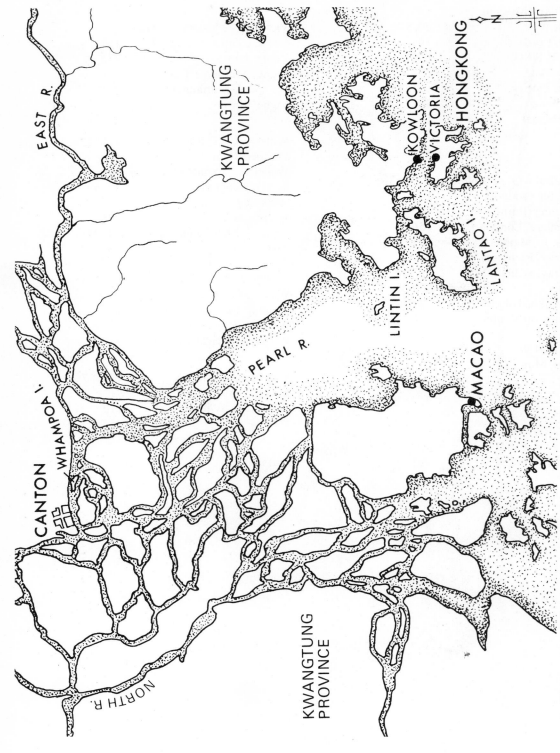

In 27 years' residence in Macau, Chinnery made a number of visits to Canton, about 70 miles to the North, and at least one visit to Hongkong, about 40 miles away. But apart from sketching trips to parts of the Pearl River delta these marked the limits of his travels in China.